## Today's Debates

# ILLICIT DRUG USE

## Legalization, Treatment, or Punishment?

Richard Worth and Erin L. McCoy

New York

Published in 2019 by Cavendish Square Publishing, LLC
243 5th Avenue, Suite 136, New York, NY 10016

Copyright © 2019 by Cavendish Square Publishing, LLC

First Edition

No part of this publication may be reproduced, stored in a retrieval system, or transmitted in any form or by any means—electronic, mechanical, photocopying, recording, or otherwise—without the prior permission of the copyright owner. Request for permission should be addressed to Permissions, Cavendish Square Publishing, 243 5th Avenue, Suite 136, New York, NY 10016. Tel (877) 980-4450; fax (877) 980-4454.

Website: cavendishsq.com

This publication represents the opinions and views of the author based on his or her personal experience, knowledge, and research. The information in this book serves as a general guide only. The author and publisher have used their best efforts in preparing this book and disclaim liability rising directly or indirectly from the use and application of this book.

All websites were available and accurate when this book was sent to press.

Library of Congress Cataloging-in-Publication Data

Names: Worth, Richard, author. | McCoy, Erin L., author.
Title: Illicit drug use : treatment or punishment? / Richard Worth and Erin L. McCoy.
Description: New York : Cavendish Square, 2018. | Series: Today's debates | Includes bibliographical references and index.
Identifiers: LCCN 2018016140 (print) | LCCN 2018016865 (ebook) |ISBN 9781502643308 (ebook) | ISBN 9781502643292 (library bound) | ISBN 9781502643285 (pbk.)
Subjects: LCSH: Narcotic laws--United States--Juvenile literature. | Narcotic laws--United States--Criminal provisions--Juvenile literature. | Drugs of abuse--Law and legislation--United States--Juvenile literature. | Drugs--Law and legislation--United States--Juvenile literature. | Drug abuse--United States--Juvenile literature. | Drug control--United States--Juvenile literature. | Drug addicts--Legal status, laws, etc.--United States--Juvenile literature. | Drug addicts--Rehabilitation--United States--Juvenile literature.
Classification: LCC KF3890 (ebook) | LCC KF3890 .W67 2018 (print) | DDC 362.29/15610973--dc23
LC record available at https://lccn.loc.gov/2018016140

Editorial Director: David McNamara
Copy Editor: Rebecca Rohan
Associate Art Director: Alan Sliwinski
Designer: Ellina Litmanovich
Production Coordinator: Karol Szymczuk
Photo Research: J8 Media

The photographs in this book are used by permission and through the courtesy of: Photos credits: Cover Tek Image/Science Photo Library/Getty Images; p. 4 Claire Galofaro/AP Photo; p. 9 U.S. Customs/Hulton Archive/Getty Images; p. 12 Timur Laykov/Shutterstock.com; p. 18 Matthew Micah Wright/Lonely Planet Images/Getty Images; p. 20 Ian Thomas Jansen-Lonnquist/The Washington Post/Getty Images; p. 21 Jonathan Newton/The Washington Post/Getty Images; p. 24 Joe Cavaretta/Sun Sentinel/ZUMA Press Inc./Alamy Stock Photo; p. 26–27 Armando Franca/AP Photo; p. 30 Internet Archive/Flickr.com/14597359068/CC PD; p. 35 Library of Congress/Wikimedia Commons/File:5 Prohibition Disposal (9).jpg/CC PD; p. 39 Dan Farrell/New York Daily News/Getty Images; p. 42 Hulton Archive/Getty Images; p. 46 Raul Arboleda/AFP/Getty Images; p. 49 Drug Enforcement Administration/Wikimedia Commons/File:Crack street dosage.jpg/CC PD; p. 52 Chief Petty Officer Brandyn Hill/U.S. Coast Guard; p. 58 Joaquin Sarmiento/AFP/Getty Images; p. 61 Noah Friedman-Rudovsky/Bloomberg/Getty Images; p. 64 Luka TDB/iStock; p. 70 Prison Policy Initiative/Wikimedia Commons/File:Lifetimechance.jpg/CC BY-SA 3.0; p. 73 ZUMA Press Inc./Alamy Stock Photo; p. 76 Rena Schild/Shutterstock.com; p. 81 Sarah L. Voisin/The Washington Post/Getty Images; p. 85 Tom Dodge/The Columbus Dispatch/AP Photo; p. 88 David Goldman/AP Photo; p. 92 Kevin D. Liles/AP Photo; p. 96–97 Gabe Souza/Portland Press Herald/Getty Images; p. 98–99 Tech. Sgt. Mark R. W. Orders-Woempner/U.S. Air Force; p. 102 zimmytws/Shutterstock.com; p. 108 March Nighswander/AP Photo; p. 112–113 Joe Raedle/Getty Images.

Printed in the United States of America

# CONTENTS

Introduction . . . . . . . . . . . . . . . . . . . . . . . . . . . . . . . . . . .5
**Chapter One:** Controversies in the War on Drugs . . . . . . . . . . . . . . . . . 13
**Chapter Two:** A History of Drugs in America. . . . . . . . . . . . . . . . . . . 31
**Chapter Three:** Stopping the Flow of Drugs. . . . . . . . . . . . . . . . . . . 53
**Chapter Four:** Drug Offenders in Prison . . . . . . . . . . . . . . . . . . . . 65
**Chapter Five:** The Legalization Debate . . . . . . . . . . . . . . . . . . 77
**Chapter Six:** Addiction Treatment and Harm Prevention . . . . . . 89
**Chapter Seven:** Drugs and Constitutional Rights . . . . . . . . . 103
Glossary . . . . . . . . . . . . . . . . . . . . . . . . . . . . . . . . . 116
Further Information . . . . . . . . . . . . . . . . . . . . . . . . . 118
Bibliography . . . . . . . . . . . . . . . . . . . . . . . . . . . 122
Index. . . . . . . . . . . . . . . . . . . . . . . . . . . . . . . . . 140
About the Authors . . . . . . . . . . . . . . . . . . . . . . . 144

# INTRODUCTION

"**P**eople are dropping like flies," says Steve Williams, mayor of Huntington, West Virginia, "and it makes no difference what their economic status is. They could be wealthy, they could be mired in poverty … This scourge takes no prisoners."

The scourge Williams is talking about has spread throughout the United States, but has had a particularly devastating impact on his community. He's talking about the opioid epidemic.

## A Deadly Habit

Opioids are a type of drug used for pain relief that can be either prescribed by a doctor in pill form or illegally distributed as the drug heroin or in other

*Opposite:* Huntington, West Virginia, is experiencing an opioid epidemic, and many of the drugs may have been distributed in and around public housing projects.

forms. They are highly addictive and can lead to overdoses and even death. Between 2000 and 2012 in the United States, hospitalizations related to opioid use increased 72 percent. About 115 Americans die each day as the result of an opioid overdose. The US Department of Health and Human Services calls the growing misuse of opioids an epidemic, and in October 2017, the White House declared it a public health emergency.

The city of Huntington, West Virginia, has ten times the national average of overdose deaths. More than one in ten babies there are born suffering symptoms of opioid withdrawal. On August 15, 2016, there were twenty-eight overdoses in just one afternoon.

Now, Huntington is fighting back. In early 2017, local authorities in Cabell County, where Huntington is located, decided to sue ten distributors of pharmaceuticals, accusing them of distributing prescription drugs for "illegitimate medical purposes." Among those companies being sued are Kroger, AmerisourceBergen, and Cardinal Health, all among the nation's largest distributors of prescription drugs. Huntington has also teamed with other West Virginia cities to sue the Joint Commission, a nonprofit organization that accredits thousands of health organizations and hospitals around the country, for allegedly spreading misinformation about opioid addiction and the dangers associated with it, and for its financial ties to pharmaceutical companies.

"Most of the heroin addiction that we have began with individuals who had a prescription with pain medication, and that prescription led to an addiction," Williams explains. "Huntington is a town of just under 50,000 people. Our county is 96,000 people. Yet over a five-year period, just a five-year period, there were 40 million doses of opiates that were distributed in this county alone." In the United States as a whole, about 64,000 people died of a drug overdose in

2016, a 19 percent increase from 2015 and the largest one-year increase in the history of the country. West Virginia, with 41.5 overdose deaths per 100,000 residents, had the highest rate of overdose deaths in the United States in 2015.

One former drug addict in Huntington attests that it was easy to obtain prescription opioids. He would simply go to the doctor complaining of a back injury, pay in cash, and walk away with a prescription. Indeed, the sheer number of prescriptions being written is a primary factor in the increase in drug addiction and abuse in the United States. According to an analysis published in the *Morbidity and Mortality Weekly Report*, about three times as many opioids were prescribed in 2015 as in 1999. The quantity of prescriptions varied widely around the country.

The city of Huntington argues that drug distributors are also to blame. "We need to go to those who are complicit in causing the epidemic and they need to be held accountable," Williams says. "If you've been able to have record profits, then invest in healing people that have found themselves injured by your product."

In response to the lawsuit, one company told the BBC, "We intend to vigorously defend ourselves in this litigation while continuing to work collaboratively to combat drug diversion." John Parker, a representative for a trade association of drug distributors, argued that distributors are just the middlemen: "Distributors don't write prescriptions. We don't dispense medicines to patients, and we don't regulate the practice of medicine or pharmacy in any way."

By March 2018, five executives from the McKesson Corporation, a pharmaceutical company, were expected to be questioned under oath as part of the suit. The company stood accused of offering commissions or bonuses to those employees who succeeded in increasing opioid sales. McKesson has denied awarding such bonuses.

Meanwhile, as of early 2018, eleven local governments around the state of West Virginia had joined Cabell County in suing drug distributors.

## Illegal Drugs and the Law

Even when a drug is prescribed to someone, the misuse of that drug—taking more than is prescribed, sharing the drug with others, or using the drug to "get high"—can involve or lead to illegal behavior. Once a person has become addicted, he or she may attempt to obtain more drugs illegally, or even commit crimes such as theft in order to pay for such drugs. Misusing prescription drugs is dangerous, especially in the case of highly addictive drugs such as opioids or benzodiazepines (drugs prescribed for insomnia or anxiety).

While some drugs are legal with a prescription, others are entirely illegal, as is the case with heroin (an opioid), cocaine, and methamphetamines (commonly called "meth"). Using or selling these addictive drugs is illegal throughout the United States. Yet the question of which drugs should be illegal has become a matter for debate. Marijuana has been legalized for medical use in twenty-nine states and for recreational use in nine states. Yet it is still illegal on the federal level, leading to a slew of legal complications. Proponents for its legalization argue that it is not as dangerous as heroin, cocaine, or even alcohol, which is legal; they also point out that its legal sale might decrease the amount of dangerous and violent illegal trafficking of the drug and reduce the number of people in American prisons. However, many argue that it is a gateway drug, meaning that it leads to further drug use.

The current policies on which drugs are legal and illegal—or illicit—arose during the early twentieth century. Federal legislation outlawed certain types of drugs, such as heroin and cocaine. During the 1970s, President Richard Nixon declared a War on Drugs to combat the growing abuse of illegal drugs as well as their increased importation and sale. The Controlled Dangerous Substances Act of 1970 classified a variety of drugs according to their harmfulness, addictive qualities, and medical uses. Some, such as morphine, could be used under strict medical supervision, but many other drugs—including heroin, cocaine, marijuana, and LSD—were established as completely illegal. Anyone caught using or selling these drugs faced a prison sentence.

Since that time, law enforcement officials have scored some impressive successes in stopping the importation of illegal drugs into the United States. Nevertheless, large quantities of drugs

US Customs patrol officers remove hundreds of pounds of marijuana discovered near the US-Mexico border in 2000.

Introduction 9

continue to be smuggled across US borders. In response, federal and state governments have passed harsh sentencing guidelines to imprison those caught possessing or selling illegal drugs. The Supreme Court has supported efforts by law enforcement officials to search those suspected of possessing or selling drugs. Prisons have filled up with drug offenders, but after these offenders serve their sentences and are released, a high percentage return to prison again. As a result, some experts argue that imprisoning drug users is ineffective. They propose that some drugs, such as marijuana, should be legalized, and more time and resources should be spent on the prevention of drug use and the treatment of drug addicts.

Meanwhile, many have questioned the role of pharmaceutical companies and doctors in potentially exacerbating the current epidemic of prescription drug misuse. Pharmaceutical companies have a powerful influence on federal lawmakers and have spent nearly $2.5 billion on lobbying and campaign contributions in the last decade. In April 2016, a bill called the Ensuring Patient Access and Effective Drug Enforcement Act was passed. Some say the law prevents the Drug Enforcement Administration (DEA) from halting many questionable drug shipments initiated by drug distributors, who have been making billions of dollars on such shipments. For years, the DEA had been trying to investigate these transactions, in which many distributors were selling prescription pills under suspicious conditions. The DEA had wanted to crack down on such sales. The pharmaceutical industry reportedly spent more than $100 million on lobbying to secure the passage of the Ensuring Patient Access and Effective Drug Enforcement Act.

Meanwhile, law enforcement and lawmakers continue to face a variety of challenges. A relatively new drug is now claiming thousands of lives. Deaths from overdoses of fentanyl, a synthetic opioid that's cheaper to produce than heroin, increased by 540 percent in the three years leading up to 2016. In 2015, it claimed 20,100 lives—more than heroin or prescription opioids. Maryland, Kentucky, and Delaware were the states hardest hit by this new epidemic. Many drug users don't take fentanyl intentionally; rather, it's mixed in with other drugs without their knowledge, and because fentanyl is several times more powerful than heroin, it can be easy to overdose.

*STAT*, a publication that specializes in the life sciences and medicine, predicted in 2017 that as many as 650,000 people would die of opioid overdoses over the next ten years—especially if fentanyl and other synthetic opioids remain popular and if wait times for treatment in the most-affected states, such as West Virginia, don't improve.

## Chapter One

# CONTROVERSIES IN THE WAR ON DRUGS

As the illicit drug trade continues to flourish, US policy makers are seeking more effective ways to fight back. Trade will often cross state lines and US borders, in which case it falls under the jurisdiction of the Drug Enforcement Administration (DEA). In 2016, the top five districts for drug-trafficking offenders in the country were along the US-Mexico border. Meanwhile, local law enforcement and fire departments throughout the country respond regularly to calls for medical assistance and reports of drug-related crime or violence.

Many believe that imprisonment is the fair punishment for illegal drug use or trafficking. After all, they argue, it is generally the go-to punishment

*Opposite:* Two major components of the War on Drugs focus on anti-drug education in schools and heavier sentences for offenses committed in or near schools.

for breaking any other serious law in the United States; why should there be an exception for drug-related offenses? However, some insist that addiction treatment is a better way of addressing the problem at its source. Others argue for the legalization or decriminalization of some drugs and point to the decrease in marijuana trafficking offenses since 2012, when the states of Colorado and Washington legalized recreational use of the drug. (Several more states would legalize it in the years afterward.) In order to understand each of these arguments, it's essential to know more about changes in drug abuse over time, how drugs are trafficked, what role prisons play, and where previous policies have succeeded and failed.

## Anti-Drug Legislation in the United States

During the nineteenth century, drug abuse in the United States grew slowly. Opium was imported from Asia by the British and then sold in the United States, where some people smoked it in so-called opium dens. During the Civil War, doctors in northern hospitals used opium and morphine as painkillers; some soldiers, however, later became addicted to them. Small amounts of these drugs were also added to medicines prescribed by doctors for adults and children. In 1914, in response to the increasing use of opium and other narcotic drugs such as cocaine and heroin, the US Congress passed the Harrison Narcotics Tax Act, outlawing the nonmedical importation and sale of many of these substances.

During the 1930s, the newly established Federal Bureau of Narcotics led a successful effort to prohibit the use of many drugs, including marijuana. A number of laws passed from the 1950s through the 1970s imposed harsher sentences on anyone caught using or selling illegal drugs. In the early 1970s, President Richard Nixon announced the War on Drugs, aimed at eliminating the supply of illegal drugs and reducing their use. Laws passed during the 1980s, such as the Anti-Drug Abuse Acts of 1986 and 1988, increased expenditures aimed at stopping the sale of crack cocaine and increasing prison sentences for users and dealers of heroin, cocaine, and other illegal drugs.

These laws currently guide police officials and law courts in the twenty-first century. Since President Nixon started the War on Drugs in 1971, the federal effort to stop the supply and use of illegal drugs has grown into a program costing about $20 billion annually. An additional $25 billion is spent each year by state and local governments. The United States has also spent billions of dollars trying to destroy coca crops in the Andes Mountains of South America; coca is the plant that produces cocaine.

## Trafficking and Drug Busts

In July 2008, US Customs agents operating along the Mexican border in Nogales, Texas, seized a large load of illegal heroin weighing forty-seven pounds. It had been carried in a car across the border with Mexico, one of the main sources of the heroin that reaches the United States. Heroin is an opiate—a painkiller—which is highly addictive and illegal in the United States. Heroin is produced from opium poppies, and large fields of these poppies grow in the Durango and Sonora regions of Mexico, as well as in Colombia in South America, and Afghanistan in Asia.

Police and federal officials had also led raids on smugglers bringing in other types of drugs from across the border, such as cocaine. Heroin, however, was relatively inexpensive. As in 2008, heroin still costs only about $10 for an amount that will get a person high—significantly cheaper than opioid pills, which can sell for $80 apiece. This is why many people who get addicted to prescription pills eventually turn to heroin to feed their addiction, so that with the rise in opioid addiction, heroin overdoses have increased too.

The US and Mexican governments have teamed up to fight back against drug production and trafficking. The Merida Initiative is a program designed to undercut transnational criminal organizations by strengthening border controls, improving resources for investigation and prosecution, and working to decrease the demand for drugs. In 2014 alone, the Mexican government seized more than 929 metric tons (1,024 tons) of marijuana, 3.6 metric tons (3.9 tons) of cocaine, 19 metric tons (20 tons) of methamphetamine, and 424 kilograms (934.8 pounds) of heroin. It also shut down 143 meth labs and extradited sixty-six people to the United States to face criminal charges.

About the same time that US Customs agents were seizing smuggled heroin in Nogales, agents of the DEA had discovered more than seven thousand marijuana plants growing in the Cleveland National Forest near San Diego, California. Established in the early 1970s, the DEA is one of the primary federal agencies (along with US Customs and Border Protection) charged with eliminating the supply of illegal drugs. According to the DEA, the marijuana was worth more than $20 million in sales to drug traffickers. Together with the San Diego Sheriff's Department, the DEA not only removed the marijuana plants but also found the camp where the traffickers were living while they tended their crop. As Special Agent in Charge Ralph W. Partridge said after the raid, the "DEA will continue to work [with other agencies] to protect our natural resources from the contamination and damage caused by drug traffickers' illicit use of our public lands."

In 2016, the state of California legalized the recreational use of marijuana by adults twenty-one and older, as well as the properly licensed cultivation of marijuana. The law, commonly called Proposition 64, also permits some people who were previously convicted of marijuana-related offenses to be resentenced—or even to have such offenses removed from their records. "The dysfunction and dark side of this underground economy has gone to such an extent that people are ready for change," argued state representative Jared Huffman, referring to the dangerous illegal trade of marijuana. Supporters of the law argue that legalizing marijuana prevents drug-related crimes and violence, allows its quality to be more carefully controlled, and permits it to be taxed, potentially resulting in $1 billion in new tax income for the state every year. Proponents also argue that it makes expensive drug busts and imprisonment unnecessary—although cultivation on federally owned land, as in the case of the Cleveland National Forest bust, remains illegal.

## The Debate

Efforts to address the problem of illegal drugs in the United States have yielded a variety of approaches, each with its supporters and detractors.

In recent years, the majority of US adults have expressed concern over the large prison population and support for alternative approaches to the War on Drugs. A 2016 poll released by the Pew Charitable Trusts found that 61 percent of registered voters believed that there are too many drug offenders in US prisons; most expressed a desire to dedicate more prison space to violent offenders and terrorists. Similarly, the American Civil Liberties Union Campaign for Smart Justice reports that in a national opinion poll, 68 percent of Americans said they'd be more likely to vote for a candidate who supported reducing prison populations and rededicating the money saved to mental health and drug treatment programs. Six in ten said that drug addicts who commit serious crimes belong in such rehabilitation programs, not in prison.

Some experts have called for legalizing drugs, especially marijuana, which is the most widely used illegal substance.

Demonstrators convene in support of the legalization of marijuana in Huntington Beach, California.

However, others claim that this will increase drug use and send the wrong message about substance abuse, especially to children.

Harm reduction—that is, efforts to reduce the dangers associated with drugs, even in cases where drug use continues—is another option, but far less money is spent on this alternative than on drug busts. Some apparently successful efforts, including needle exchanges, methadone programs, and drug substitution treatment, have faced strong opposition.

Treatment, such as drug rehabilitation programs, has also proven to be effective against drug abuse. But again, far more energy and financial resources have been put into the War on Drugs than into drug-treatment programs.

Law enforcement officials and the courts have usually supported strong measures under the law to combat drug trafficking and drug use. However, these measures, such as searching people suspected of possessing drugs, may have eroded certain fundamental rights protected under the US Constitution.

## Does Prison Work?

Drug busts like those in Nogales and San Diego are one of the weapons used by US government officials as well as local and state law enforcement agencies to deal with the illegal-drug problem. People caught using, manufacturing, and selling illicit drugs are often sentenced to prison. The Anti–Drug Abuse Act of 1986 included mandatory minimum sentences for those found guilty of using or selling illegal drugs. Judges—some of whom might have imposed lenient sentences on people involved in drug-related activities, especially using drugs—no longer had much discretion in sentencing. In 2016, the average sentence in the United States for a drug offender was ninety-four months if the person was convicted of a crime with a mandatory minimum penalty, forty-two months if not.

Corey Taylor was released from prison in 2007 after being convicted of selling drugs. Following his release, he returned to Houston, Texas, where he lived with his grandmother. Many of his friends had also been sent to prison for drug-dealing. "Out of 10 of my partners [in dealing drugs], only one is doing anything different," he told Solomon Moore of the *New York Times*. "I have some friends I haven't seen for 10 years because either I was locked up or they were locked up."

Mark Wright and Al Jarreau Davis were also released after going to prison for drug possession. Wright admitted that almost everyone he knew, including his brother, had gone to prison for drug-related crimes.

Although he had been in prison for ten years, Wright had no sooner been released than he returned to selling drugs. "I was bred into this life," he told Moore. "It's survival of the fittest

The Nashua, New Hampshire, police department's narcotics unit arrests a woman for alleged heroin possession in 2017.

out here." Davis followed the same course as Wright, selling cocaine and marijuana to support himself after he was released.

In 2018, nearly 2.3 million Americans were in state and federal prisons and local jails—about 20 percent of them for drug-related offenses. Opponents of imprisonment as a long-term solution to the drug epidemic point out that it leads to prison overcrowding. The population of state prisons throughout the United States has grown by 700 percent since the 1970s, and in the last twenty years, state corrections budgets have increased nearly four times over. Total spending as reported by forty-five states in 2015 was $43 billion per year, or an average of $33,274 per inmate.

Opponents also say that prison doesn't get to the root of the problem, which is the addiction that drives people to commit crimes. The data seem to support this argument, given that the majority of drug offenders will commit another crime after they've been released. The rate of recidivism—or rearrest after conviction or release from detention—among federally convicted drug traffickers was 50 percent over an eight-year period, according to a 2017 report from the United States Sentencing Commission. Five-year recidivism among all drug offenders nationwide is even higher, at 76.9 percent. To break this cycle, prison authorities and community agencies across the United States have turned to drug-treatment programs.

## Drug-Abuse Treatment and Harm Reduction

In 2016, the National Survey on Drug Use and Health reported that about twenty-one million people (7.8 percent of the population over age twelve) needed treatment for substance abuse. Yet only about 3.8 million of these people actually received any help at a treatment facility in 2016. The reasons varied from not having any health insurance to not being ready to go into treatment. Yet the National Institute on Drug Abuse has estimated that one dollar

A counselor (*left*) leads an addiction counseling session at a state prison in Utah in 2015.

Members of Stop the Organized Pill Pushers Now (STOPPnow) demonstrate against a pain clinic in Dania Beach, Florida, in 2010.

the Commission on Combating Drug Addiction and the Opioid Crisis pointed out that overprescribing was a serious problem, adding that health professionals need to be better educated about methods for treating pain.

In July 2017, the US Department of Justice charged 120 people with crimes related to opioids—including doctors who were reportedly operating "pill mills," facilities where it is particularly easy to obtain prescriptions for painkillers. "Too many trusted medical professionals, like doctors, nurses, and pharmacists, have chosen to violate their oaths and put greed ahead of their patients," said Attorney General Jeff Sessions.

*Vox* reports that during the 1990s, some pharmaceutical companies pushed doctors to prescribe more opioids, hoping to boost their profits. Overprescribing led to an increase in addiction and more pills available for sale on the street. Efforts to discourage this and to crack down on pill mills has led to a steady decrease

# The War on Drugs and the Constitution

As a result of the War on Drugs, since the 1980s, many cases have come before the US Supreme Court that involve the Fourth Amendment to the Constitution. This amendment prevents an individual or his or her residence from being searched by the police without a warrant—that is, without permission to search—issued by a court. Many of these cases have involved searches by police or school officials who suspected that individuals may be using or dealing drugs, but who did not have warrants. In close 5–4 and 6–3 decisions, Supreme Court justices have taken markedly different positions in favor of, and opposed to, allowing these searches.

Some of these decisions have applied to students in schools. Searches without warrants of students or their lockers have been permitted if a school official has a "reasonable suspicion" that a student possesses an illegal drug. A majority of justices allowed this exception in order to protect discipline and prevent crime in the classroom. However, some justices dissented, arguing that it was a violation of the Fourth Amendment. Court rulings have also been applied to student athletes and young people involved in sports or other extracurricular activities who were suspected of using drugs.

in prescriptions for opioids since 2010. However, there were still three times more opioids prescribed per person in 2015 than in 1999.

## Legalization

Some Americans have asked whether legalization or decriminalization of some drugs might effectively address problems associated with illegal drugs in the United States. The answer might be found by taking a look at other countries' drug policies. In parts of the Netherlands, for example, marijuana has been decriminalized—that is, people are allowed to smoke it without being arrested, even though it still technically illegal. Portugal decriminalized all drugs in 2001, after which, the *Guardian* newspaper reports, "Rather than being arrested, those caught with a personal supply might be given a warning, a small fine, or told to appear before a local commission—a doctor, a lawyer and a social worker—about treatment, harm reduction, and the support services that were available to them." Portugal has since seen a dramatic decrease in deaths by overdose, problematic drug use, crime linked to drugs, incarceration rates, and even hepatitis and HIV rates—though not all these changes can be credited exclusively to the policy change.

A drug addict (*left*) in Lisbon, Portugal, exchanges used needles for new ones. Portugal's drug-addiction bureau helps addicts find treatment.

Some experts in the criminal justice field believe that the United States is not winning the War on Drugs and should consider the legalization of some substances, especially marijuana. Twenty-four million people are currently marijuana users—a number that continues to increase especially as it has been legalized in some states—according to the 2016 National Survey on Drug Use and Health conducted by the Substance Abuse and Mental Health Services Administration. Proponents of legalization argue it saves time and money now spent by police officers and law courts arresting and prosecuting marijuana users. Moreover, they argue that marijuana is effective for certain medical uses, such as reducing pain for cancer victims undergoing chemotherapy to fight their disease. Twenty-nine states have legalized it for medical purposes; nine have legalized it for recreational use.

Organizations such as the American Medical Association have contended that marijuana is a gateway drug—a drug that introduces or encourages the use of more harmful substances—and argue that its legalization will have a negative impact, especially on young people. However, according to a study published in the *American Journal of Psychiatry* in 2006, the vast majority of marijuana users do not use other illegal drugs.

Opponents of legalization warn that laws permitting the use of marijuana may also be the first step in legalizing all substances that are currently illegal—a "slippery slope" that isn't worth risking. They also contend that the demand for any drug will increase if it is legalized. Indeed, in states where marijuana has been legalized, demand is up. "On the recreational side of the business, the originally legalized states are still posting massive growth," Chris Walsh, editor of *Marijuana Business Daily*, reported in 2017.

The DEA also argues that the United States should pursue a policy of zero tolerance on drugs, meaning that the use of illicit drugs such as marijuana, cocaine, and heroin should not be tolerated. In 2015 alone, the agency destroyed more than four million marijuana plants being grown within US borders and confiscated 4,300 weapons from people growing marijuana, also known as cannabis. "Marijuana is the only major drug of abuse grown within the US borders," the DEA's website reports. "The DEA is aggressively striving to halt the spread of cannabis cultivation in the United States."

In January 2018, Attorney General Sessions announced that the federal government would strictly enforce federal antimarijuana laws, even in those states where the drug has been legalized. He said the measure would provide US attorneys with "all the necessary tools to disrupt criminal organizations, tackle the growing drug crisis, and thwart violent crime across our country." This undercut a 2013 Justice Department policy that shielded much of the burgeoning legal marijuana industry from legal troubles. That policy, announced during the Barack Obama administration, had announced that federal enforcers would focus on prosecuting anyone selling marijuana across state borders or to minors, and on situations involving organized crime or gangs. In light of Sessions' policy change, Jasmine Taylor of Human Rights Watch concluded, "The war on drugs, whether it went away or just slowed down, is now back."

## Chapter Two

# A HISTORY OF DRUGS IN AMERICA

**B**efore highly addictive substances such as cocaine were illegal in the United States, they were widely used and even prescribed. It took the establishment of new laws aimed at protecting the public's safety to raise awareness about the dangers surrounding many now-illicit drugs.

## Dangerous Medicine

An advertisement for Mrs. Winslow's Soothing Syrup that appeared in 1888 explained that it would soothe the ache in a child's mouth while he was teething. Mrs. Winslow's syrup was so effective because it contained morphine—a powerful narcotic made from opium

*Opposite:* A page from a 1908 World Almanac advertises Mrs. Winslow's Soothing Syrup, which was actually an addictive narcotic.

that relieved pain. Dr. Birney's catarrhal powder, advertised about the same time, guaranteed relief from catarrh—an inflammation of the mucous membranes in a patient's nose and throat. Dr. Birney also claimed that his powder would cure colds, hay fever, headaches, and even deafness. The powder's most powerful ingredient was a 2-to-5 percent dose of pure cocaine—a highly addictive drug.

During the late nineteenth century, patent medicines—as these products were called, because the formulas were owned by the manufacturer—were regularly used by hundreds of thousands of Americans to provide relief from a variety of aches and pains. No laws required the medicine manufacturers to list the ingredients in their products or to prove that they actually did what they claimed to do. The main ingredient was frequently a powerful drug that deadened pain and did little else.

Among the most popular drugs was laudanum. This was liquid opium combined with alcohol that was often prescribed by doctors for women who suffered from depression. After American playwright Eugene O'Neill was born in 1888, his mother, Ella, was suffering from pain and depression and received laudanum and morphine, also derived from opium, from her doctor. Eventually, she became addicted—an experience that O'Neill later described in his play, *Long Day's Journey into Night*. "I hate doctors," the mother in the play cries as she suffers from the effects of morphine addiction. "They'll do anything … to keep you coming to them. They'll sell their souls. What's worse, they'll sell yours, and you never know it until one day you find yourself in hell."

During the late nineteenth century, some doctors believed that the only way to cure morphine addiction was to offer a substitute: cocaine. The white powder, produced from the leaves of South American coca plants, could easily be sniffed through the nose by patients who used it. Cocaine also seemed to offer an effective cure for depression. The famous detective Sherlock

Holmes, a fictional character created by British author Sir Arthur Conan Doyle, regularly injected a 7 percent solution of cocaine into his arm. Only gradually did doctors begin to realize that cocaine—like morphine—led to severe addiction in patients who took the drug.

In 1898, the Bayer Company of Elberfeld, Germany, introduced another drug made from morphine, which was called heroin. In its advertising, Bayer claimed that heroin was effective in treating coughs, hay fever, colds, and pneumonia. Less than ten years later, doctors discovered that patients using heroin developed serious addictions and suffered from severe withdrawal symptoms when they stopped using the drug. By this time, an estimated seventy million Americans were taking patent medicines that contained habit-forming drugs. About 250,000 were opiate addicts and 200,000 were cocaine addicts, according to author Jill Jonnes.

In 1905, journalist Samuel Hopkins Adams published a series of articles in *Collier's* magazine titled "The Great American Fraud." These articles exposed the fraudulent claims of patent medicines. Adams belonged to a group of journalists called muckrakers. They included writers such as Upton Sinclair, who achieved fame by exposing unsanitary conditions in the meatpacking industry. The work of the muckrakers helped to persuade the US Congress to pass the Pure Food and Drug Act in 1906. Among other things, this legislation required patent medicines to identify the drugs contained in them. As a result, these drugs were taken out of some medicines, while others went off the market.

The Pure Food and Drug Act, however, did not put an end to the use of dangerous drugs. Doctors continued to write prescriptions for cocaine and morphine to combat pain. Finally, Congress enacted the Harrison Narcotics Act in 1914. This law required doctors and druggists who dispensed opiates and cocaine to fill out special forms issued by the government, which could now keep track of what was being used and for what purposes. The government interpreted the Harrison Act to mean that doctors could no longer prescribe an opiate, such as morphine, to maintain a patient who already had an addiction. In part, the law was also aimed at Chinese immigrants, some of whom were suspected of illegally importing opium from China. The government's position was upheld in 1919 by the Supreme Court in a case involving Dr. Charles Doremus of San Antonio, Texas. Dr. Doremus had provided morphine pills to one of his patients who was an addict. The court said that this violated the Harrison Act.

Addicts were now faced with a stark choice—they could either stop using cocaine or heroin, or find an illegal supplier for the drugs. Not only were the drugs not available, but the few clinics that treated substance abusers were also closed. The US government had begun a policy of zero tolerance for illegal drugs.

## Prohibition and Beyond

At about the same time, Prohibition came into effect with the passage of the Eighteenth Amendment to the US Constitution in 1919. The sale and manufacture of alcohol was now outlawed in the United States. To enforce the law, the federal government established a Prohibition Unit in the Treasury Department. As part of this unit, the government set up a Narcotics Division, which began arresting anyone who violated the antidrug laws. According to author Jill Jonnes, "violators were swelling the prison rolls." At one federal prison, nearly half of new inmates in 1923 "were drug act violators, and of these, 299 were addicts."

Prohibition did not stop the sale and manufacture of alcohol. Instead, it was supplied illegally, often by criminal gangs that manufactured alcohol at secret locations in the United States or imported liquor from abroad, where it was still legal. Many Americans went to bars and nightclubs, known as speakeasies,

New York City officials oversee agents as they pour liquor into a sewer after a raid during Prohibition.

where alcohol was served illegally. Local police knew that the speakeasies existed but they were often bribed by the owners to "look the other way," and not close them.

Like illegal speakeasies, the underground drug trade thrived as well. Criminal gangs led by men such as Arnold Rothstein—a finely dressed gangster who rode in a chauffeur-driven Rolls-Royce—made many millions of dollars supplying illegal drugs to people who wanted them. In some cases, these substances were purchased through American drug companies. Drugs like morphine were still manufactured for medical purposes, such as for use in surgery as a painkiller. The drug manufacturers then set up fake companies in Mexico and Canada, and the gangsters purchased drugs that were sent there, bringing them illegally into the United States. New legislation passed in the early 1920s that closed down these fake companies. However, gangsters were also importing drugs from pharmaceutical firms in Europe, where

A History of Drugs in America    35

there were fewer restrictions on the sale of heroin or cocaine. On top of that, congressional investigations had exposed corruption in the Bureau of Narcotics.

In 1930, the independent Federal Bureau of Narcotics was established with a new commissioner, Harry Jacob Anslinger. When Anslinger became head of the Federal Bureau of Narcotics, there were an estimated one hundred thousand substance abusers in the United States. Illegal opium was being grown and manufactured into narcotics in Turkey, or shipped to France and Germany for manufacture, then smuggled into the United States. Anslinger sent agents to Europe whose mission was to work with local law enforcement officials and paid informants to identify drug shipments and seize them before the drugs could be sold in the United States.

That same year, the United States and more than fifty other nations, primarily in Europe, signed an agreement called the Limitation of the Manufacture of Narcotic Drugs. Under the terms of this agreement, each country carefully monitored the quantity of narcotics made from opium being used for strictly medical purposes. If this did not match the amount being produced, then each nation was required to reduce the supply. As a result, the amount of legal opium being produced was cut by almost 85 percent to 8,000 tons annually.

The availability of illegal drugs in the United States declined during the 1930s. At the same time, treatment clinics began to be built once again. In 1935, the federal government opened a new treatment center in Lexington, Kentucky, followed three years later by another facility in Fort Worth, Texas. By the early 1940s, the impact of treatment and the work of the Federal Bureau of Narcotics had reduced the number of opiate addicts to about forty thousand.

# Harry Anslinger (1892–1975)

Born in 1892 in Altoona, Pennsylvania, Harry Anslinger was one of nine children. His father, Robert, was a barber from Bern, Switzerland, and his mother, Christiana, was born in Baden, Germany. Harry later remembered that at the age of twelve, while visiting a neighbor, he heard a woman addicted to morphine yelling to her husband that she needed to get a supply of the drug from the local pharmacy. The man told Harry to go to the drugstore and bring back the morphine. As a teenager, he also witnessed the death of a pool player who smoked opium. These experiences would go on to influence his opinion on the sale and use of such drugs.

Anslinger attended Pennsylvania State College and was employed as an investigator on the Pennsylvania Railroad. Later, he went to work for the US Department of State and was assigned to Hamburg, Germany. During the 1920s, he intercepted ships taking liquor into the United States in violation of the Prohibition laws, as well as a vessel carrying illegal drugs. Eventually, Anslinger was reassigned to Nassau in the Bahamas, an archipelago in the Caribbean. Alcohol was passing from Great Britain, through these islands, and into the United States, and Anslinger convinced the British government to put a stop to the traffic.

Eventually, he was promoted to assistant commissioner in the Prohibition Bureau and, finally, head of the narcotics operation in 1930. He would hold this position for the next thirty-two years until his retirement, leading the effort to stop the flow of illegal drugs into the United States.

## Hepsters and Beats

During Prohibition in the 1920s, Harlem—a primarily African American section of New York City—became a popular destination for people looking for a jazz club or a speakeasy. Well-known jazz musicians, such as Duke Ellington and Louis Armstrong, as well as singers like Bessie Smith, performed nightly in these clubs. In the early 1930s, the Great Depression put 25 percent of American workers out of work and fewer people could afford to go to Harlem. In 1933, Prohibition was repealed, and the speakeasies closed. Nevertheless, jazz musicians continued to play their music in New York and other cities. They were known as hepsters—people who had abandoned the conventional middle-class lifestyle for a life of creativity and freedom.

Hepsters were defined in part by their fondness for drugs—especially heroin and marijuana. Made from the leaves of the hemp plant, which was also used to make rope, marijuana was smoked in New Orleans as early as 1910. It was imported primarily from Cuba and Mexico. As jazz musicians who played in New Orleans began moving north to Chicago and Harlem, they brought marijuana with them. Marijuana had not been banned by previous drug laws, but states gradually began to pass laws against marijuana use during the early 1930s. Articles began appearing in magazines claiming that the use of marijuana led to violent crimes. In 1937, Harry Anslinger wrote an article in the *American Magazine* titled "Marijuana: Assassin of Youth." Nevertheless, many doctors, as well as the American Medical Association, believed that marijuana had legitimate uses to help patients deal with problems such as severe migraine headaches.

In 1937, Congress passed the Marijuana Tax Act. This required any person who grew or sold marijuana to register with the government and pay a tax on the product. Since every state had outlawed marijuana, it meant that growers and sellers could

Poet Allen Ginsberg, who was open in his work about experimentation with drugs, reads to a crowd in New York City in 1966.

immediately be identified and arrested, although this usually did not happen. Marijuana continued to be popular among hepsters, or hep cats, as they were also called during the 1930s and 1940s. It was considered a natural part of the jazz scene—a symbol of independence and creativity. However, other people used marijuana as well.

Another group of unconventional people were known as hipsters, beatniks, or Beats. The Beat Generation was a term coined by author Jack Kerouac, who published his classic novel, *On the Road*, in 1957. Based on his own experiences, the book described the travels of his main characters across the United States as well as their experiences with drugs. The Beats believed that drugs could open up new avenues toward creativity. Kerouac himself was a heavy user of alcohol, marijuana, and another drug, a stimulant known as Benzedrine. He often wrote while high on drugs.

The Beats regarded themselves as people who were beaten down by middle-class life, steady jobs, and conventional families. Like the hepsters, they rebelled and chose a more independent lifestyle. The Beats included not only Kerouac but other writers, such as poet Allen Ginsberg.

The Beats exemplified an alternative lifestyle that seemed to have a special appeal to young people. Some of them had already begun experimenting with drugs, and they were searching for a way of life that was different from that of their parents. Meanwhile, the number of heroin addicts was growing, and the drug was becoming more easily available in New York City as well as in other communities. Although Anslinger and the Bureau of Narcotics claimed to be handling the drug problem, more and more drugs were entering the United States and the bureau wasn't doing enough to stop the flow. At the same time, some of the bureau's agents had been stealing drugs seized in raids and engaging in their own trafficking operations. Investigations into the bureau during the 1960s revealed that about sixty out of three hundred bureau agents had been involved in drug trafficking. The extent of the corruption helped convince Harry Anslinger to resign from his position as head of the bureau because he seemed unable to stop this activity and feared for his own reputation.

## 1960s Drug Culture

In August 1969, a giant traffic jam extended for miles outside the tiny village of Bethel, New York, about forty miles from the town of Woodstock. Approximately four hundred thousand young people were heading there for the biggest rock concert of the decade. Even the heavy rains did not lessen their enthusiasm during the three-day event, as they listened to performances by stars including Janis Joplin, Jimi Hendrix, and Joan Baez. But the audiences who camped out in the fields during the Woodstock festival had not only come for the music. They were also there to participate in an event that symbolized a new youth culture, which had emerged during the 1960s. Illegal drugs such as marijuana were openly used by many of the people who attended the music festival. As one local resident recalled, it may have been a "four-day wallow in … drugs and rock 'n' roll but it's part of American culture, whether you like it or not."

The music festival that came to be known as Woodstock occurred at the end of one of the United States' most tumultuous decades. In 1963, President John F. Kennedy had been assassinated in Dallas, Texas. Five years later, his brother, Senator Robert F. Kennedy, was killed in Los Angeles, California, while he was running for the Democratic presidential nomination. That same year, the Reverend Dr. Martin Luther King Jr., a leader of the civil rights movement aimed at ending discrimination against African Americans, was murdered in Memphis, Tennessee.

Meanwhile, the United States had become involved in an unpopular war in Southeast Asia against the communist government of North Vietnam. On college campuses throughout the United States, students were protesting the Vietnam War and the fact that many thousands of them were being drafted—compelled by federal law—to serve in the army. For some, drugs became a way to escape from the unpleasant realities of life during the 1960s. They adopted Timothy Leary's slogan, "Turn on! Tune in! Drop out!" Leary was a former Harvard professor who championed the use of the drug lysergic acid diethylamide (LSD). LSD was used by such cultural icons as poet Allen Ginsberg, and even people in government, as a way to achieve enlightenment and gain new insights about themselves.

According to the Bureau of Narcotics, an increasing number of young people in high school and college were experimenting with LSD. The drug is a hallucinogen that causes users to experience startling visions. Easy and inexpensive to produce, LSD was widely available to anyone who wanted to try it. What many users didn't realize was that some people never recovered from taking LSD and landed in intensive psychiatric care or committed suicide after using it.

Meanwhile, heroin abuse was rising, especially among residents of poor neighborhoods in many American cities. As the price of a dose of heroin rose from five to twenty-five dollars during the 1960s, crime also began to increase, with addicts committing more and more burglaries and muggings to pay for their addictions. In the South Bronx section of New York City, murders during the 1960s rose by 500 percent. Many residents who were not drug abusers were scared by the violence and crime but still tried to live normal lives. Drug overdoses were also rising in America's major cities.

In 1969, newly elected President Richard Nixon announced that the number of young people arrested for drug use had risen by 800 percent from 1960 to 1967. Drugs had become a "growing

Music fans sit on top of a painted bus at the August 1969 music festival Woodstock, where drug use was widespread.

menace to the general welfare of the United States," he said. "It is doubtful that an American parent can send a son or daughter to college today without exposing the young man or woman to drug abuse. Parents must also be concerned about the availability and use of such drugs in our high schools and junior high schools." The president pointed to the rising number of arrests among teenagers who were using or selling drugs. He launched a new initiative against drug abuse, partly aimed at cutting off the supply.

Part of this initiative included reducing the influx of heroin. Members of his administration met with leaders in Turkey, where opium was grown, and France, where it was manufactured into heroin, urging them to shut down the illegal flow of drugs. Though the French and Turkish leaders made promises, little happened.

Congress also enacted the Controlled Dangerous Substances Act of 1970, which set up so-called schedules of drugs—rankings based on how dangerous or addictive they were and on their medical value. Schedule I drugs included heroin and LSD, which had no medical uses and were extremely harmful and addictive. Using these drugs for any purpose was considered a criminal offense, and dealers of heroin or LSD were to be given stiff prison sentences. Schedule II included drugs that had some medical uses but could only be taken under a doctor's supervision. On this list were drugs such as morphine and cocaine. Schedules III through V included drugs that were less likely to be abused. Marijuana, for instance, was considered less dangerous than drugs like LSD and heroin; those caught smoking marijuana therefore received only a short sentence in jail or a fine. In addition to the schedule classifications, the act authorized law enforcement officials to seize the property of individuals suspected of being involved in drug trafficking and to sell that property.

# The War on Drugs

In 1971, President Nixon announced the War on Drugs. Over the next few years, heroin use began to decline, as police increased their efforts to round up drug traffickers and schools launched new drug-abuse prevention programs. However, as heroin use dropped, other types of drug abuse increased. According to the National Household Survey of Drug Abuse, the number of young people ages twelve to seventeen smoking marijuana rose from 7 percent in 1971 to 16.7 percent in 1979. There was also an increase in the number of people ages eighteen to twenty-five using cocaine—from 3.1 percent in 1974 to 9.3 percent in 1979.

## The Cocaine Trade

During the 1970s, cocaine—a relatively expensive drug—became increasingly popular among more affluent Americans. Articles in popular magazines claimed that cocaine users could avoid the terrible addiction that affected heroin users. Cocaine use was chic, according to an article in *Newsweek* magazine in 1977, which added that the drug "is not addictive and causes no withdrawal symptoms. Taken in moderation, cocaine probably causes no significant mental or physical damage and … it can be safer than liquor and cigarettes when used discriminately." However, the *Newsweek* article was based on inadequate science and overlooked the problems with cocaine use that had cropped up during the nineteenth century.

The article also did not mention that cocaine, as well as marijuana, was being smuggled into the United States by Latin American drug gangs. During the 1970s, murders in the area of Miami, Florida—a center of drug smuggling from Latin America—rose as these gangs battled to control the drug trade. Drug busts by law enforcement agencies had also increased. In a report to Congress, a DEA official stated during the late 1970s that "South Florida has become inundated with marijuana and cocaine smuggling and trafficking … It is not unrealistic to say that the smugglers are better equipped, have more resources and financial backing than the entire law enforcement community."

Meanwhile, scientific studies had begun to show the dangerous side effects of cocaine abuse. The more often people used cocaine, the more dependent on the drug they became. Some users reported deep psychological problems, while others said that they had been forced to steal money to support their drug addiction. Then, in 1986, star basketball player Len Bias—who had just joined the Boston Celtics team—died of a heart attack caused by cocaine. This made cocaine overdose a national issue.

Nevertheless, the growth in the cocaine traffic continued. At first, criminal gangs from Chile purchased coca leaves, turned them into cocaine at secret laboratories, and then transported it to Florida, where it was often sold by Cuban traffickers. Soon, Colombian gangs began to move in on the cocaine business. Murders in Florida increased during the late 1970s and early 1980s as Colombians battled Cubans for control of the drug traffic, which had been increasing since the 1960s. It is important to note that these massive trafficking operations arose because there was a high demand among Americans for the drugs they were producing and selling.

The Colombian gangs were based around the city of Medellín in Colombia, where they had built a large, secret laboratory facility on an island in one of the country's rivers. In 1984, the Colombian government launched a raid on the facility, where they captured a large quantity of cocaine and an arsenal of weapons. The cocaine traffickers, though, had escaped before the police arrived. In retaliation, the Medellín cartel murdered the Colombian minister of justice. A year later, the traffickers launched an attack on the Colombian justice department, killing twelve of the country's federal justices. They were sending a message to the judges of Colombia: do not convict any members of the cartel—or

*Colombian workers destroy a coca plantation in the mountains northeast of Medellín in 2014.*

extradite them (that is, send them to the United States for trial and imprisonment). The US government had an agreement with Colombia that called for drug traffickers to be sent north for trial in American courtrooms.

The violence continued during the early 1990s until Colombian police killed or captured many of the cartel's leaders; others were extradited to the United States. However, their place had already been taken by another group called the Cali cartel, headquartered in the Colombian city of Cali, which smuggled cocaine into the United States. They, too, were eventually arrested by Colombian police.

In the meantime, the DEA was trying to stop heroin traffic from Afghanistan and Pakistan, where opium poppies were grown. They had agents working closely with the Pakistani government trying to round up drug traffickers, but the flow of heroin did not decrease.

## Anti-Drug Legislation

During the 1980s, the US Congress passed a series of laws designed to strengthen the effort against drug trafficking. The Comprehensive Drug Penalty Act of 1984 improved certain provisions of the 1970 Act. It was now easier for law enforcement officials to seize the property of people suspected of being involved in drug trafficking. The paperwork was reduced, and the property that was seized could be sold much more rapidly, providing additional funds to finance the War on Drugs.

The Controlled Substance Analog Enforcement Act of 1986 tried to close a loophole relating to so-called designer drugs. These were substances, such as the newly created hallucinogen ecstasy, that had not been listed on the schedules of the 1970 legislation. The new act stated that if the drug produced similar effects to one already on a particular schedule, it too would be added to that schedule. Ecstasy, for example, became a Schedule I drug, the most dangerous type.

In 1986, Congress passed legislation imposing mandatory minimum sentences. These were especially aimed at drug dealers. The guidelines were designed to punish traffickers who might otherwise get off with light sentences if the judge hearing their case decided to be lenient. The sentences range from five years to life imprisonment depending on the number of prior convictions and the amount of drugs the individual charged in the case was dealing. For example, a defendant caught with 220 pounds of marijuana would be eligible for a minimum sentence of five years in prison. A defendant received a minimum of ten years in prison if he or she was caught with at least 1.1 tons (1 metric ton) of marijuana.

The reason for these harsh sentences was that the defendants were not just users of marijuana, but clearly dealers based on the large quantities of drugs in their possession. Dealers could reduce their sentences if they gave evidence that assisted law enforcement officials in capturing other drug traffickers. However, those possessing certain types of drugs were also subject to mandatory minimum sentencing. For example, an individual possessing 5 grams (0.18 ounces) or more of crack cocaine was subject to a sentence of five years behind bars for the first offense. These sentences increased for second and third offenses.

Another act, passed in 1988, increased funding for the War on Drugs and established the Office of National Drug Control Policy, which was tasked with coordinating efforts to deal with drug trafficking and drug abuse. It was also aimed at combating a new form of cocaine that had been entering the US market. Called crack cocaine, it consisted of cocaine crystals that could be smoked instead of cocaine powder that was sniffed.

## The Crack Epidemic

Crack cocaine began entering the United States in the 1980s. Crack crystals, or rocks, were smoked—"freebased"—through a water pipe. By smoking the drug instead of snorting it, the effects were felt much faster. A freebaser could develop an expensive habit in just a few weeks or months, while those who snorted cocaine powder took much longer—two to five years—to develop that type of habit. Freebasers also used far more cocaine than snorters to feed their habit, so dealers could make much more money selling crack to them instead of powdered cocaine.

Indeed, the number of cocaine users was beginning to decline from a high of twenty-two million in the early 1980s. People had seen its effects on their friends and decided that the drug should be avoided. However, as powdered cocaine use decreased, crack hit the streets and a drug epidemic broke out. Crack was inexpensive, with a rock costing as little as two to five dollars. It became especially popular in some of the poorer neighborhoods

Crack cocaine is a fast-acting and more addictive version of powder cocaine. Its use became widespread in the United States in the 1980s.

in large cities. People began using crack when they were teenagers and selling the drug to support their habit. Turf wars broke out among crack traffickers, and murder rates increased in cities such as New York and Washington, DC. Pregnant women who used crack passed on serious problems to their newborn babies, who were born with problems such as intellectual disabilities and cerebral palsy—a disease that damages the brain, affecting a child's ability to speak and move his or her arms and legs.

During the 1980s, the administration of President Ronald Reagan had launched an antidrug campaign using the slogan "Just Say No," which was created by First Lady Nancy Reagan. At the same time, President Reagan was committed to shrinking the size of the federal government and the expense of running it. Therefore, his administration cut funding for antidrug programs. However, as the drug problem worsened, public pressure mounted to do something about it. The 1988 Anti–Drug Abuse Act vastly increased the funds being spent in law enforcement efforts led by the DEA. The next year, President George H. W. Bush appointed a so-called drug czar to run the newly established Office of National Drug Control Policy.

Then, in December 1989, the president launched an invasion of Panama, in Central America, called Operation Just Cause. The invasion overthrew Panamanian dictator Manuel Noriega, who was accused of endangering the lives of American citizens living in Panama. He also allegedly permitted Panama to be used as a stopping-off point for drug cartels. The drug traffickers had been shipping illegal substances, such as crack and powdered cocaine, from South America through Panama to the United States.

Arrests of drug traffickers in the United States had risen from 103,000 in 1980 to more than 400,000 by 1989. As efforts to combat drug abuse increased, crack use began to decline in major cities like New York. However, people continued using it in smaller cities and towns. American society also had to deal with a number of families that had been torn apart by crack use and young children afflicted with illnesses because their mothers had used crack while they were pregnant.

## A Shift in the War on Drugs

Despite the great efforts that had been made to stop them, drug cartels in the 1980s remained powerful, smuggling large quantities of crack and other illegal substances into the United States. Cocaine flowed from Latin America—especially Colombia, Peru, and Bolivia. Poppies grown in Afghanistan and Myanmar supplied most of the world's heroin-manufacturing operations. Finally, in the late 1980s, the Soviet Union collapsed, and the nations in Eastern Europe and Central Asia that had been part of its empire became independent. Some of them, such as Poland, became sources of illegal drug manufacturing and sales.

During the 1990s, the US War on Drugs remained a top priority. But President Bill Clinton, elected in 1992, shifted the emphasis from battling drug traffickers to treating drug abusers. However, as drug abuse, especially among teenagers, continued to rise, the administration shifted tactics again. President Clinton appointed a new drug czar, General Barry McCaffrey, and made him a member of the president's cabinet. Along with more staff, the drug czar now had greater power to fight the War on Drugs. During the 1990s, the US government stopped 1.3 tons (1.43 metric tons) of heroin from entering the country, according to author Thomas C. Rowe, an expert on the illegal drug problem and author of *Federal Narcotics Laws and the War on Drugs*. In addition, the Clinton administration worked with nations in South America to spray coca crops and destroy them. Nevertheless, coca continued to be grown in Colombia, Peru, and Bolivia to feed the demand for cocaine. Despite some successful efforts in the War on Drugs, drug manufacturers and drug dealers still produced and sold their products.

Today, the conversation about drug abuse includes discussions of treatment options in addition to approaches to criminal prosecution and international collaboration. Efforts to battle drug use are complicated all the more as governments and regulators seek to curb drug trafficking across and within US borders.

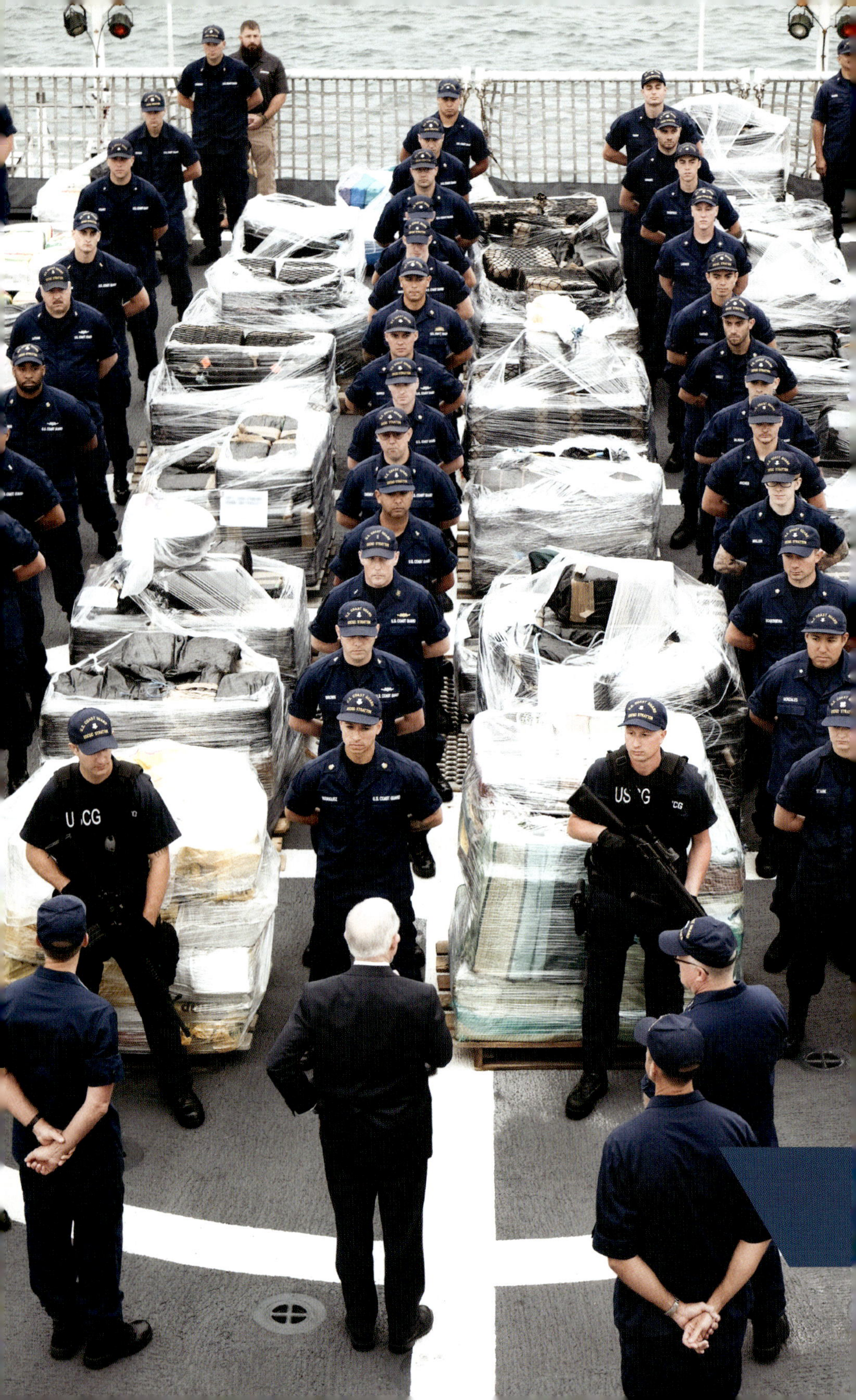
USCG

## Chapter Three

# STOPPING THE FLOW OF DRUGS

In June 2017, the US Coast Guard's San Diego, California, sector made an unusual Facebook post: "Here's what 18 tons of cocaine look like!" it read. The post was accompanied by photos and video of cranes lifting huge pallets of cocaine from a ship. The drugs, which had a street value of half a billion dollars, had been confiscated over the past three months in the eastern Pacific Ocean along the South and Central American coasts. Fifteen drug-smuggling ships had been intercepted during that time. Still, this 36,000-pound (16,329-kilogram) haul comprised less than 9 percent of all the cocaine the Coast Guard had intercepted in 2016.

## Intercepting Smuggled Drugs

A major part of the War on Drugs involves keeping illegal substances from entering the United States. Several agencies are involved in this effort, including

*Opposite:* Attorney General Jeff Sessions (*foreground, center*) speaks to the crew of the Coast Guard cutter *Stratton* as they unload tens of thousands of pounds of seized cocaine in California in 2017.

the US Coast Guard, which tries to prevent drugs from reaching the United States by sea. Immigration and Customs Enforcement (ICE) examines luggage carried by travelers as well as vehicles as they enter the United States through airports and across the borders with Mexico and Canada. The Drug Enforcement Agency (DEA) is also involved in stopping the movement of drugs into the United States, as are the Federal Bureau of Investigation (FBI) and the Office of National Drug Control Policy.

US Customs and Border Protection (CBP) reported in March 2018 that, on a typical day, CBP seizes 5,863 pounds (2,443 kg) of narcotics. The DEA is also involved in seizures and arrests related to smuggled drugs. Some of the seizures come as a result of joint efforts with other governments. For example, a cooperative program with the Netherlands has led to the arrests of drug traffickers involved in smuggling ecstasy into the United States, according to the Office of National Drug Control Policy. Another case involved Canadian drug manufacturers in British Columbia who were producing a powerful form of marijuana called "BC Bud." In a joint operation with the Canadian Mounted Police, ICE and other US agencies arrested forty smugglers and seized their illegal drugs—8,000 pounds (3,629 kg) of BC Bud, and 800 pounds (363 kg) of cocaine, which was $1.5 million worth of the illegal drug. The law enforcement agencies also seized three airplanes used to transport the drugs. Called Operation Frozen Timber, the project began in 2004. In all, more than forty arrests were made. The drug traffickers intended to bring their drugs into the northwestern United States and California.

Mexico, meanwhile, has been a leading source of marijuana, heroin, methamphetamine, and cocaine, drugs that are smuggled across the border into the United States. Under President George W. Bush, the federal government initiated a program called the Southwest Border Counternarcotics Strategy to increase the number of border-control guards. Their mission was to tighten security along the border and to reduce the amount of illegal drugs brought into the United States. In addition, the Mexican government, under the leadership of President Felipe Calderón, who was elected in 2006, sent out a large force of about seven thousand federal troops who arrested members of violent drug gangs. Under President Barack Obama, the strategy expanded to include support for border communities that have been badly affected by the drug trade.

Reducing the supply of drugs has led to some success in tackling the illegal drug problem. Nonetheless, large quantities of illegal drugs still enter the United States. According to the Office of National Drug Control Policy (ONDCP), in the early twenty-first century, efforts to stop the flow of illegal drugs resulted in seizing only about 6 percent of the heroin entering the United States. One reason is the demand for heroin and other illegal drugs. The 2016 Survey on National Drug Use and Health reported that the number of heroin users had risen from 136,000 in 2005 to 948,000 in 2016. Cocaine use had also increased from 900,000 in 2002 to 1.9 million people in 2016. Increasing demand has meant a larger and larger market for illegal drugs.

The money to be made in illegal drugs is also great enough for traffickers to continue manufacturing and smuggling these substances into the United States. A 2017 Global Financial Integrity report stated that the global illegal drug market was worth between $426 and $652 billion annually. Marijuana comprised the largest submarket, at 43 or 44 percent of the total.

The task of stopping these drugs from entering the United States seems to be far greater than law enforcement officials can achieve. US Customs and Border Protection processes more than a million passengers and pedestrians every day, in addition to 283,664 privately owned vehicles and 78,137 rail, truck, and sea containers. Checking all the baggage carried by these people or all of these vehicles is impossible.

In addition to drugs coming from outside the United States, other illegal substances are produced domestically. For example, methamphetamine, a highly addictive stimulant, is produced in secret laboratories throughout the United States. Much of the marijuana sold in the United States is grown in the country in secret locations, many of them in California. Federal law prohibits the production of marijuana in every state, and though some states permit licensed cultivation of the crop, they can still clash with federal institutions on matters of policy. Although law enforcement officials find some of these locations and destroy the crops, new ones soon take their places. Many growers cultivate marijuana indoors, where the plants are harder to spot. In addition, marijuana grown indoors can be produced year-round with as many as a half-dozen harvests annually. This increases the supply of marijuana inside the United States. As a result, marijuana is readily available to many Americans, including teens. What's more, these drugs are often sold by young people themselves.

## Crop-Eradication Strategies

In 2000, the Clinton administration initiated Plan Colombia, a coordinated effort with the Colombian government to eliminate the production of cocaine and heroin. Over the next seventeen years, the United States would invest $10 billion into such initiatives as improving Colombian law enforcement programs, which are aimed at hunting down and stopping the drug cartels that are terrorizing the country. Under the George W. Bush administration, the United States began the Andean Counterdrug Initiative, which spent over $700 million annually. In 2003, some of these funds were used by Colombians to spray about 50,000 square miles (129,499 sq km) of coca crops from airplanes with herbicide as well as about 1,000 square miles (2,590 sq km) of poppy fields. In Bolivia, thousands of farmers received funds to stop growing coca and switch to other crops. Another program, called Air Bridge Denial, was begun in 2003 and led to the destruction of several planes carrying drugs as well as the seizure of large amounts of cocaine in Colombia.

At the time, the *New York Times* reported, "Colombia's armed forces have severely weakened the Revolutionary Armed Forces of Colombia (FARC) guerrillas, a major player in the drug trade." The FARC had used the money made on the sale of heroin and cocaine to fund its terrorist activities aimed at overthrowing the Colombian government. In 2012, peace talks between the FARC and the government began, and in 2014 they agreed to work together to fight drug trafficking. In 2016, they signed a ceasefire; the FARC agreed to stop trafficking narcotics, and the disarmament of FARC rebels began the next year. However, as the FARC extricates itself from the cocaine business, many have worried that "FARC's absence could also create a vacuum that any number of other criminal groups already in the jungle may seek to fill, giving rise to more violence," as J. Weston Phippen put it in a 2016 article in the *Atlantic*.

However, some elements of the program have failed, according to author Michael Shifter. Part of the program was aimed at eradicating coca crops grown by Colombian farmers by spraying them with herbicides (crop killers) and substituting them with another crop. "Current policy instruments are simply unable to match the power of market forces; coca may be effectively eradicated in one area, only to pop up in another," writes Shifter. The reason is that, even though growing coca is illegal in Colombia, farmers can make more money growing coca than any other crop. Much of the coca has been sold to terrorist groups such as the FARC or the National Liberation Army (ELN), another organization that has tried to undermine the Colombian government. The ELN and the Colombian government have also undergone exploratory talks, and in 2017 a temporary truce was announced.

Ironically, Colombia has seen a boom in coca production since the FARC laid down its arms. With the government offering cash incentives to rural communities that stop growing coca, these

*FARC guerrilla fighters in Colombia prepare for peace as they march to a Transitional Standardization Zone in April 2017.*

communities "know that the best way to get the government's attention and ensure it follows through on development promises is to have coca in the ground, so they are planting more and more in anticipation of qualifying for official payments," Nick Miroff wrote in the *Washington Post*. However, until that happens, both Colombia and countries to which cocaine is exported face a new challenge: in 2016, there were more than 460,000 acres (188,000 hectares) of coca being cultivated in Colombia, a 141 percent increase from 2012, when 192,742 acres (78,000 ha) were in production. This boost in supply has decreased the price of cocaine and in turn fueled more cocaine use in the United States: "US officials say the flood of cheap Colombian product is so large that it has quietly created its own demand," according to Miroff.

Crop-eradication strategies have also been implemented in Afghanistan, which produces about 70 percent of the world's opium, according to a 2016 report from the United Nations. During the 1990s, the Taliban came to power in Afghanistan after the overthrow of a regime backed by the Soviet Union (modern Russia). The Taliban government may have used the money from opium sales to support its government. It had also been allied with al-Qaeda—the terrorist organization that masterminded the attack on the United States on September 11, 2001, killing more than three thousand Americans. In retaliation for this attack, the Taliban was overthrown later in 2001 by a US-led invasion; the Taliban, however, remains an influential faction in the country today. Although a new government has taken power in Kabul, the capital of Afghanistan, the production of poppies has continued. The Afghan government's efforts to eradicate the opium crop in Afghanistan have included providing alternative seeds and fertilizer, implementing development projects, and destroying the crop. These efforts, however, have not been very successful, in large part because opium poppies are so much more lucrative than other crops. Many farmers also say they haven't received the support they were promised.

In fact, according to Congressman Steven Kirk of Illinois, Osama bin Laden, former head of al-Qaeda, used money from trafficking heroin sourced from Afghanistan to finance his operations. "We now know al-Qaeda's dominant source of funding is the illegal sale of narcotics," Kirk said in 2004. Thomas Schweich, a member of the George W. Bush administration who was involved in the War on Drugs in Afghanistan, added that post-Taliban Afghan president Hamid Karzai may also have involved in the drug trade; Karzai, he said, had been "playing us like a fiddle: The US would spend billions of dollars on … improvements; the US and its allies would fight the Taliban (whose guerrilla forces have been attacking the government); Karzai's friends would get rich off the drug trade."

Today, fighting opium cultivation in Afghanistan is still an important strategy for combating terrorism. In 2017, political risk analyst Anders Corr explained that, to fight off the Taliban and the Islamic State—another terrorist group—in Afghanistan, it is necessary to eradicate opium production in the Nangarhar province, where both groups are active. Poppy production there increased 43 percent between 2015 and 2016. Destroying this market "will deny its use for financing to both the Taliban and Islamic State." Corr recommended a multipronged strategy for eradicating opium

# Coca and Cultural Heritage in Bolivia

President Evo Morales of Bolivia, elected in 2006, declared that he would work with the United States in the effort to stop the production of cocaine in his country—but not to stop the production of coca. Coca has long been used for medical purposes (such as helping with altitude sickness) and as a nutritious food among indigenous populations in Bolivia. It also has religious importance. Morales, as the first indigenous president of Bolivia, has sought to protect coca production as a traditional practice in the region.

The United States has spent millions on the War on Drugs in Bolivia, working with local police and military forces. Former Bolivian administrations cooperated with the United States in these efforts, passing legislation that severely limited the amount of coca that could be grown in the country. However, Morales and many of the Bolivian people resented US interference in their country. One farmer in the Chapare region recalls how DEA-backed antinarcotics police forces would treat coca cultivators before the crop was legalized: "They would turn up suddenly, at any time of day or night, and start interrogating us—they would hit you or kick you for no reason … We used to sleep out in the open, in the coca field, so they couldn't find us."

Before becoming president, Morales was head of the coca-growers union in Bolivia. His union members rely on the income from coca to support themselves and their families. Coca was legalized in 2004, and in 2008, Morales expelled the DEA from the country after thirty people died in violent confrontations. While US president Barack Obama expressed disapproval with Bolivia's antinarcotics efforts, Morales views his country's approach as a success. The "coca yes, cocaine no" effort sets maximums for how much coca each family can produce and

Bolivian president Evo Morales is welcomed to his hometown with a necklace made of coca leaves, a traditional medicine and food.

requires that the leaves be sold at authorized markets. In 2016, Morales concluded: "We in Bolivia, without US military bases and without the DEA, even without the shared responsibility of drug-consuming countries, have demonstrated that it is possible to confront drug trafficking with the participation of the people."

In March 2017, a bill was passed that almost doubled the amount of land that could be used to legally cultivate coca leaves in Bolivia. The country's Constitutional Tribunal upheld that law in November 2017. "Our sacred leaf of coca from our ancestral culture is now valued and protected, instead of prohibited and prosecuted like in the past," Morales said in response to the ruling.

production, including careful use of aerial herbicide application, land confiscation, and giving laborers land of their own to cultivate, so that they don't work on poppy farms. Simple crop destruction, however, won't do the trick. "Current methods of manual opium poppy eradication, such as use of sticks by local officials to break the stems of poppy flowers, are a complete failure in Afghanistan. They only succeed at making the state appear to be doing something about the problem," Corr argues.

## Targeting Money Launderers

In August 2008, Steven Sodipo and Callixtus Nwaehiri were convicted of illegally selling almost ten million hydrocodone pills over the Internet. Hydrocodone is a prescription drug used as a pain reliever. It is among the growing number of prescription drugs being abused in the United States. Others include the painkiller OxyContin. Sodipo and Nwaehiri sold hydrocodone through a business called NewCare Pharmacy from 2004 through 2006. Working with website operators, the two men obtained large quantities of signed prescriptions from a few doctors, and NewCare filled the prescriptions. This permitted drug abusers to receive hydrocodone without ever seeing a doctor. The Baltimore office of the DEA investigated the operation and shut it down—one of many similar schemes stopped by the DEA.

In addition to being convicted of illegal sales of hydrocodone, Sodipo and Nwaehiri were also found guilty of money laundering. This is a process used by drug traffickers to make the proceeds from the illegal sale of drugs look legitimate. According to lawyers Bruce Zagaris and Scott Ehlers of the Drug Policy Foundation, money laundering usually involves three steps. "The first stage, placement, entails depositing the drug proceeds into domestic and foreign financial institutions. The second stage, layering, involves creating layers between the persons placing the proceeds and the persons involved in the intermediary stages, to hide their source and ownership." The money may be deposited in Mexican banks, for example, and then wired to US banks. Cash may also be smuggled across the US-Mexican border and deposited in American banks. "In the third stage, integration, the proceeds have been washed, and a legitimate explanation for the funds is created. This can be done, for instance, via front [fake] companies, false invoicing [for products that are never purchased] … or investment in real estate, tourism, and other legitimate businesses."

In some cases, US companies have done business with firms in South America that have been laundering money for drug traffickers. These South American firms import products from manufacturers in the United States using laundered money. For two decades, the federal government has taken these US manufacturers to court and, in some cases, seized the money they made from the sale of their products. The government has also "frozen the assets"—prevented the company from gaining access to the funds—obtained from selling products for laundered money.

According to the 1986 Money Laundering Control Act, money laundering is a criminal offense. Foreign bank officials or associates of South American drug dealers in the United States are often paid large amounts of money to launder the proceeds from drug sales. However, as Ehlers has pointed out, it is often hard for investigators to discover whether a bank is guilty of money laundering because there are so many millions of bank transactions.

As efforts to cut down the supply of illegal drugs and seize the money made by drug traffickers continue, the US government faces a daunting task. However, targeting money launderers remains a way to not only prosecute drug traffickers, but even— sometimes—to discover them. The DEA acknowledges that it's impossible to track all proceeds made from illicit drug trafficking, so instead, it prioritizes investigating those proceeds that can lead the agency back to the sources and suppliers of drugs.

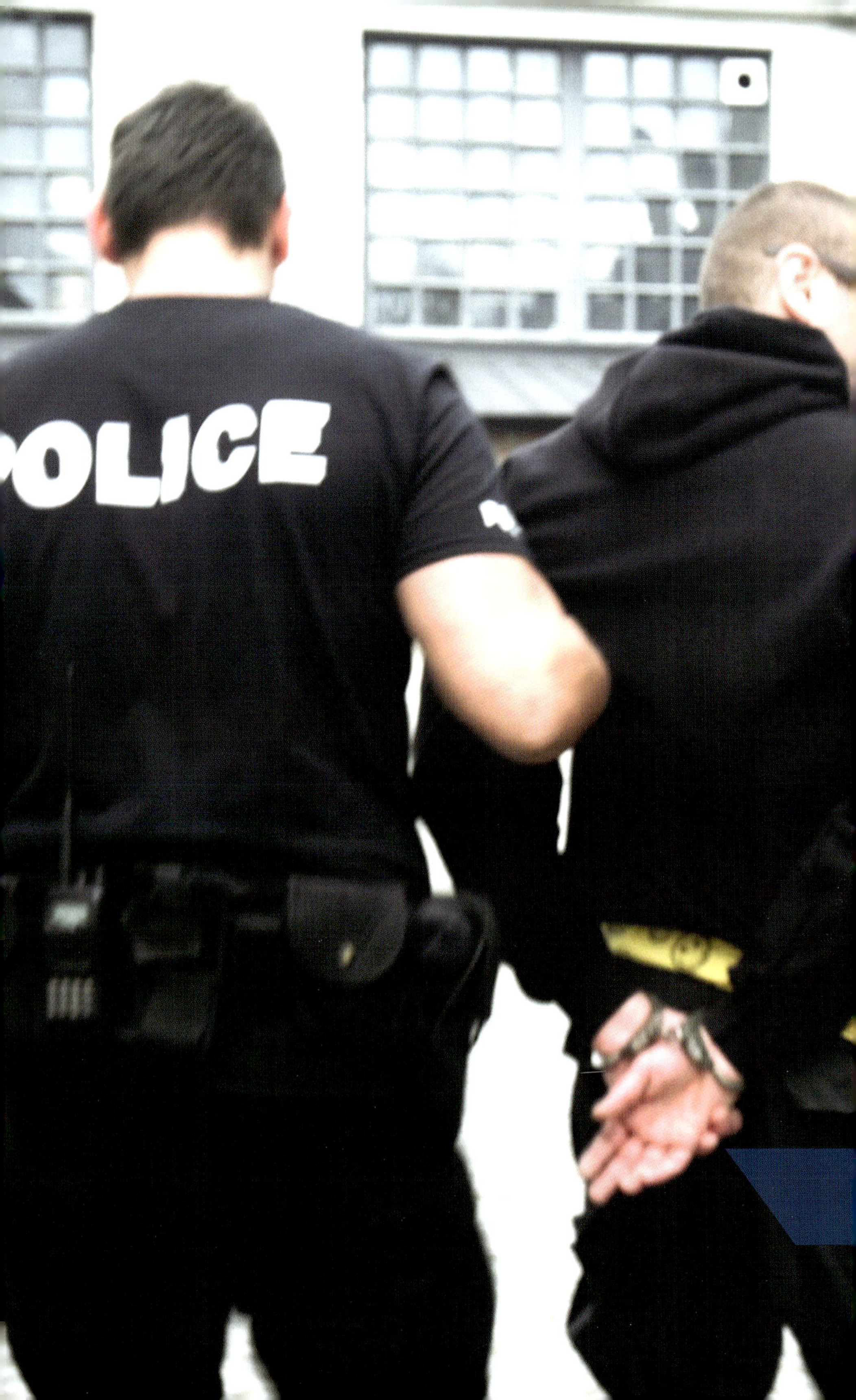
POLICE

## Chapter Four

# DRUG OFFENDERS IN PRISON

**M**ore than two million Americans are incarcerated, either in local jails or in state and federal prisons. About one in five have been imprisoned for drug-related offenses. A complicated web of policies has determined how much time a person might be incarcerated for possession, trafficking, or other drug-related crimes. Trafficking usually carries heavier sentences than possession based on the rationale that it harms more people. However, decades of policy have brought about decades of debate regarding the best approach to sentencing offenders and addressing recidivism among drug users.

## Federal Sentencing Guidelines

John Forté was a big name in music. In the 1990s, he produced albums for successful groups such as Public Enemy and the Black Eyed Peas. By

*Opposite:* Drug offenses often land people in jail or prison, but some argue that incarceration isn't the most effective way to fight the War on Drugs.

the time he was twenty-five, Forté had won a Grammy Award, the most prestigious prize in music, for the year's outstanding rap album. Many people in the music business, however, suffer through ups and downs—and Forté was no different. By 2000, he found himself short of money and needed to revive his career with a big hit. To finance a new album, he decided to accept an offer of ten thousand dollars from a man who wanted him to hire two women for a special assignment. Forté said that he thought they were supposed to be carrying cash halfway across the United States. Instead, the women were carrying large amounts of liquid cocaine. When they were arrested by police officials in Houston, the women implicated Forté, who was later arrested. In 2001, Forté was convicted of transporting drugs, and although it was the first time he had been involved in a drug crime, Forté was sentenced to fourteen years in federal prison. (President George W. Bush commuted Forté's sentence, and he was released in 2008.)

Forté's sentence was handed down by a judge who was following federal sentencing guidelines and mandatory minimum sentences. The mandatory minimums were introduced in 1973 in New York State. Under these laws, prison sentences are determined by the type of drug being used or sold, how much of the drug has been confiscated in the defendant's possession, and any prior convictions a defendant has for a drug offense. For example, the New York law carried a minimum sentence of fifteen years to life for possession of a hard drug such as heroin or cocaine.

In March 2009, the New York state assembly repealed most of the state's 1970s drug laws. As a result, judges will have much greater authority to send those arrested for drug offenses to treatment centers rather than being required to impose mandatory prison sentences. A 2015 amendment to the state's Criminal Procedure Law also facilitates this, permitting opioid addicts who are undergoing methadone therapy to participate in a diversion program. However, other states have adopted mandatory-minimum laws that were aimed at punishing drug offenses as well as other kinds of crimes. The hope was that the prospect of such heavy sentences would act as a deterrent to crime. Political leaders in each state also wanted to ensure that sentencing was not entirely left up to individual judges, who might impose vastly different levels of punishment depending on their attitudes toward particular crimes or defendants.

During the 1980s, the US Congress established a sentencing commission to set up guidelines covering federal crimes. These included offenses such as the manufacture and transport of drugs into the United States. According to author Erik Luna, a former state prosecutor and a law professor at the University of Utah, the intent of these guidelines was similar to the mandatory minimums:

> *[They] (1) promoted respect for the law; (2) offered a clear statement of purposes of punishment as well as the available kinds and lengths of sentences; (3) ensured that the offender, federal officials, and the public "are certain about the sentence and the reasons for it"; (4) met the sometimes conflicting demands of retribution, deterrence, incapacitation, and rehabilitation [and] eliminated "unwarranted sentence disparities between otherwise similarly situated criminals."*

Under the federal guidelines established in 1987, sentences are based on the severity of a crime as well as a defendant's history of offenses. Judges then use a table, based on this information, to guide them in handing down a sentence.

# Mandatory Minimums

Mandatory-minimum sentencing guidelines work in a similar way. For those prosecuted in federal cases, there is one set of mandatory minimums; for those charged at the state level, different minimums apply, and these vary state by state. For example, in Connecticut, the manufacture or sale of crack cocaine, cocaine, LSD, methadone, or heroin carries a minimum sentence of five years. Possession of a small amount of marijuana is considered a lesser crime and does not carry a mandatory minimum unless a person possesses at least 2.2 pounds (1 kg) of the drug. In many states, possession of a small amount of marijuana is considered a misdemeanor—a less serious crime. This might be punished with a prison sentence of six months to a year, or the defendant might not receive any jail time and be placed on probation—that is, supervision by a parole officer for a specific period of time.

According to Human Rights Watch, a nonprofit organization dedicated to protecting the human rights of the world's people, severe drug laws and mandatory minimums have likely been a primary factor in vastly increasing the number of US prison inmates. Between 1980 and 2014, there was a 1,000 percent increase in the number of people in prison or jail for drug-related crimes. Imprisonment during the War on Drugs has disproportionately affected African Americans, reports Jonathan Rothwell, a senior economist at Gallup, the national polling company. According to a 2014 report written by Rothwell, African Americans are less likely to sell drugs than whites, but are 3.6 times more likely to be arrested for selling drugs. Likewise, about 10 percent of both whites and African Americans use illicit drugs, yet African Americans are 2.5 times more likely to be arrested for possession. African Americans also tend to receive longer sentences for the same crimes. Today, about one in three African American males will spend time in prison at some time during their life—a number that has doubled since the 1970s.

Federal sentencing guidelines and mandatory minimums became widely used in the 1980s, while the United States was in the midst of a crack epidemic. Associated with the vast increase in crack use was a rise in violent crime, such as murder and robberies. These occurred as drug dealers battled over control of the crack market, and those addicted to crack committed crimes to pay for their addictions. According to Professor Alfred Blumstein, the increase in murders largely occurred among people age twenty-four and younger. Many of these people were unemployed and turned to dealing crack as a way to earn money. Again, efforts to battle illicit drug use disproportionately targeted nonwhite Americans. Because lawmakers and the general public incorrectly believed that African Americans were the primary users of crack, federal laws in the 1980s imposed harsher penalties for the sale or use of crack than for the sale or use of powder cocaine. "Crack cocaine was perceived as a drug of the black, inner-city, urban poor, while powder cocaine, with its higher costs, was a drug of wealthy whites," explains Jamie Fellner, formerly of Human Rights Watch. As a result, "Urban blacks, the population most burdened by concentrated socio-economic disadvantage, became the population at which the war on drugs was targeted." The Fair Sentencing Act of 2010 sought to reduce this sentencing disparity.

By the mid-1990s, the crack epidemic was declining for a variety of reasons, including the incarceration of drug offenders and the effects that incarceration had on their families. Bruce Johnson and Andrew Golub, who conducted research into drug use among young people, began to see what crack had done to the people who became addicted to it. "They clearly do not want to emulate their parents, older siblings, close relatives or other associates in their neighborhoods who were enmeshed with crack," they said. In addition, the economy improved during the 1990s, providing more jobs for young people, who then turned away from drug dealing, according to Johnson and Golub. Local police forces expanded and increased efforts to stop those suspected of dealing drugs, by taking their guns and arresting them.

Fox Butterfield of the *New York Times* reported that imprisonment may have had an impact on curbing crime. "There is no question that almost quadrupling the number of people incarcerated … has

## Lifetime Chance Of Being Sent To Prison At Current U.S. Incarceration Rates

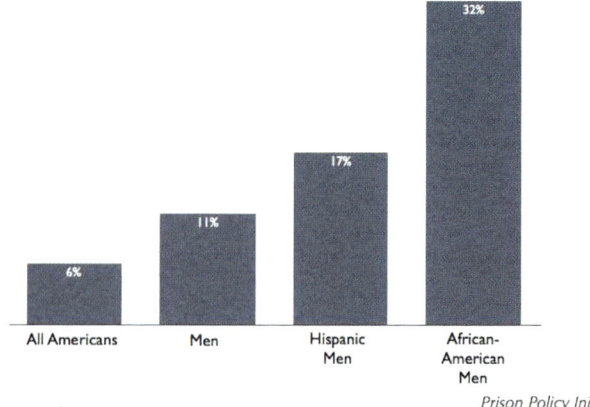

| Category | Percentage |
|---|---|
| All Americans | 6% |
| Men | 11% |
| Hispanic Men | 17% |
| African-American Men | 32% |

*Prison Policy Initiative*

Minorities in the United States are much more likely to be incarcerated, despite the fact that they are no more likely to commit drug offenses.

incapacitated many criminals and prevented many crimes." In other words, since the criminals were off the streets and behind bars, they were no longer able to commit crimes in their communities.

As the crack epidemic declined, a study appeared by the RAND Corporation—a US think tank—that focused on the impact of mandatory minimum sentences on drug offenders. Reporting on the RAND study, news network CNN stated, "Mandatory jail and prison sentences may cut consumption and crime in the short run ... But over the long run, taxpayer dollars are better spent on using standard sentencing of high-level dealers and putting heavy drug users into medical treatment programs." The study said that "treatment of heavy users would reduce about 10 times more serious crime against people and property than conventional law enforcement and 15 times more than mandatory minimums." Despite such research findings, mandatory minimums have remained in force across the United States.

Mandatory minimums have created a great deal of controversy for a variety of reasons. Tough sentences were designed to put

# United States v. Booker

In January 2005, the US Supreme Court ruled that sentencing guidelines are a violation of the US Constitution. In *United States v. Booker,* the court said that the guidelines were a violation of the Sixth Amendment, which guarantees the right to a trial by jury. According to attorney Kent Schmidt, partner in the law firm of Dorsey & Whitney, the Supreme Court decided that "the Guidelines violated the Sixth Amendment guarantee of a trial by jury by permitting federal judges to base sentencing decisions on facts never heard or decided by the jury."

Freddie Joe Booker had been stopped by police in February 2003 while he was carrying 92.5 grams (3.3 oz) of crack cocaine. He told them later that he had been selling cocaine. The jury found him guilty of intending to sell only 50 grams (1.8 oz) of cocaine. Later, the judge was presented with additional evidence indicating that Booker intended to sell 566 grams (20 oz) of cocaine. Therefore, the judge sentenced him to thirty years in prison, as stipulated by the mandatory sentencing guidelines.

Booker appealed his case, saying that the jury had never heard the later evidence regarding the sale of a larger quantity of cocaine. His appeal eventually reached the Supreme Court. In a 5–4 decision, the Supreme Court ruled that the judge had based his decision on facts never heard by the jury, and that this was unconstitutional. Further, the court said that sentencing guidelines should be advisory (a suggestion) rather than mandatory. The judge was ordered to give Booker a lesser sentence.

The US Department of Justice reported that "within only one year of the Booker decision, the number of sentences imposed within the Guidelines has dropped to 62.2 percent." Since the decision, many states that had punished drug abusers with mandatory minimum sentences have substituted drug treatment and doing work in the community.

high-level drug dealers—called "kingpins"—behind bars for a long period of time and disrupt their illegal operations. However, the US Sentencing Commission reported that only about 13 percent of the people arrested and charged are such high-level criminals. These criminals can often provide prosecutors with information that can help in the arrest of other drug offenders. Therefore, the prosecutors, in return, often reduce their sentences far below the mandatory minimums. This is permitted under the law. As a result, more than 50 percent of defendants who sell powder cocaine and more than 60 percent selling crack cocaine are "low-level offenders such as mules [couriers who smuggle in drugs on themselves] or street dealers," according to the Sentencing Commission.

A typical case is that of Elaine Bartlett of New York City, who was sentenced to twenty years in prison for carrying a four-ounce package of cocaine to northern New York. A mother of four children, this was her first offense. After sixteen years, she was finally permitted to leave prison because New York governor George Pataki gave her an early release.

# Repeat Offenders and Drug Courts

The United States has the highest incarceration rate of in any country in the world. Among those who complete their sentences and are released, about three in four drug offenders will be rearrested within five years. Given that, as Columbia University reports, just one in ten drug-addicted prisoners receives treatment behind bars, many continue to use and deal drugs when they are released and get in trouble with the law again as a result.

Mandatory minimum sentences for repeat criminals—those who commit a second or third drug offense—can be very stiff, but apparently not stiff enough to deter drug offenders. As Dr. Thomas C. Rowe, who taught for many years at federal prisons,

Pinellas County, Florida, judge Dee Anna Farnell (*left*) applauds a graduate of the We Can drug-treatment program.

pointed out, the mindset of someone convicted of a crime like drug possession is different from that of other people. For most law-abiding people, tough sentences—and the fear of getting caught—would go a long way toward preventing them from committing crimes. However, drug offenders are willing to take the risks. Drug users crave the high that they get from drugs. Drug sellers can make a large amount of money selling drugs, and they are not deterred by the threat of stiff sentences if they get caught. A prison term is just a risk they are willing to take for the money they make dealing drugs.

One alternative to imprisonment is the drug court, which began in Miami–Dade County, Florida, in 1989. Since that time, more than three thousand drug-court programs have been established across the United States. Former president George W. Bush said that "drug courts are an effective and cost efficient way to help non-violent drug offenders commit to a rigorous drug treatment program in lieu of prison." The federal government has provided extensive funding to help local communities establish these courts.

Instead of incurring a prison sentence, drug offenders enter a program that includes careful monitoring by a court and law enforcement officials as well as treatment. Many of these offenders are methamphetamine users. Meth abuse has reached "epidemic proportions," according to a report by the DEA. Under the program, offenders are expected to appear in drug court at least once a week, if not more often, for approximately three months. Each offender is also subject to frequent urinalysis tests at their homes. (Testing the offender's urine reveals whether he or she has been using drugs.) "While there, officers administer a drug test and canvas the property for signs of drug use," explained C. West Huddleston III, director of the National Association of Drug Court Professionals. "When a participant is found in violation, he or she is immediately detained and brought before the drug court judge at the earliest opportunity. When a participant is 'caught doing right' [not using drugs], the officer gives the participant positive reinforcement before leaving."

Meanwhile, the offender also receives treatment for drug addiction. Participants know that if they fail to continue treatment or return to using drugs, the court can send them back to prison. This acts as an incentive to remain drug free and stay in treatment. "I couldn't have stopped on my own. I didn't know how," said Allison Alexander, a methamphetamine user. "Drug court saved my life."

Nearly 150,000 people are enrolled in drug courts in the United States. The National Association of Drug Court Professionals reports that drug courts decrease recidivism by up to 45 percent, while family drug courts reduce the probability that children have to return to foster care by two-thirds. Special treatment courts for veterans are now helping more than thirteen thousand American veterans. And courts for people convicted of driving under the influence decrease recidivism by up to 60 percent. Drug courts also save money. When a person is sent to drug court rather than to a state prison, as much as $13,000 is saved. That's an average of $27 saved for every dollar invested in such programs.

Nevertheless, these courts are not the answer for all drug users—and some say they may not be the right approach at all. Critics argue that many reports on the success of drug courts fail to compare their outcomes with those of community-based treatment or harm-reduction programs (which include the treatment of heroin abuse with methadone or buprenorphine, less-dangerous but tightly controlled opioids). "Many drug courts mandate abstinence as a condition for participation in treatment without any basis in medical evidence. They often disallow medication-assisted treatment and punish relapse with jail," explains Christine Mehta, co-author of *Neither Justice Nor Treatment: Drug Courts in the United States*. "Methadone and buprenorphine are included in the World Health Organization's Model List of Essential Medicines. Despite their evidence-base, methadone and buprenorphine are stigmatized within large parts of the criminal justice system and treatment community as 'swapping one addiction for another.'" In the end, many drug courts fail to provide treatment that is based on what evidence has shown to be effective, Mehta argues.

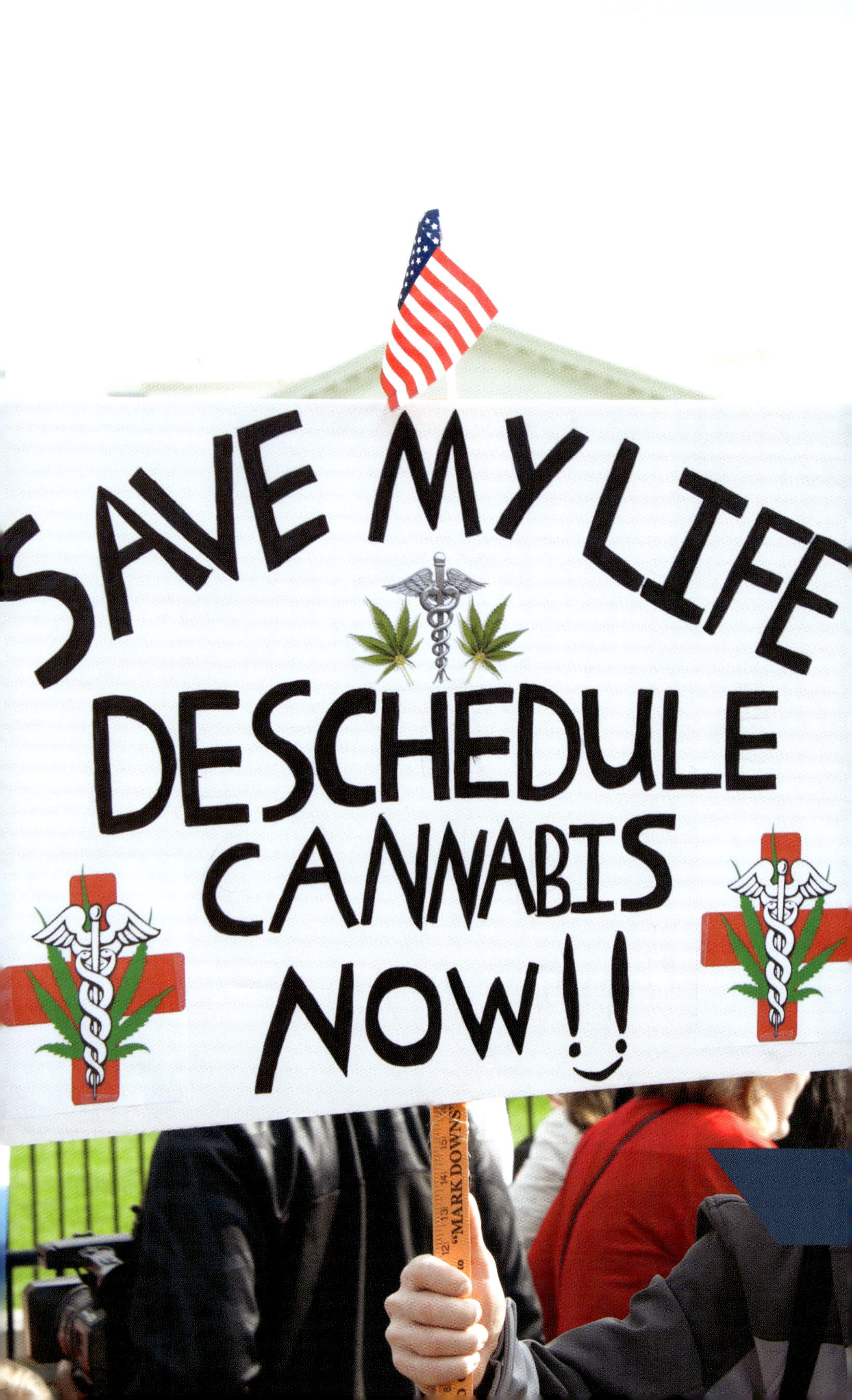
SAVE MY LIFE
DESCHEDULE
CANNABIS
NOW!!
"MARK DOWNS"

## Chapter Five

# THE LEGALIZATION DEBATE

"**Y**ou can't have a war on drugs, you can only have a war on people," retired police major Neill Franklin told the audience at a CNN town hall forum in July 2016. "And the way it's manifested itself here [in the United States], it ended up being mainly a war on black and brown people for things like mere possession of drugs, where people may have a substance abuse issue. Let me put it this way: we're attempting to solve a public health crisis with criminal justice solutions."

Franklin is the executive director of Law Enforcement Action Partnership, or LEAP (formerly Law Enforcement Against Prohibition). Founded in 2002 by five police officers, the nonprofit group has grown to more than five thousand members and has five international

*Opposite:* A protestor supports the legalization of medical marijuana in front of the White House on April 2, 2016.

chapters. More than 150 speakers for the organization gave nearly three thousand talks about alternative approaches to drug policy in 2016 alone. The organization advocates for harm-reduction treatment as well as broader law enforcement–related issues such as body cameras and allowing offenders to speak in a respectful and neutral space. It also supports ending drug prohibition and releasing drug offenders while offering treatment and raising awareness about the dangers of drugs. However, it is not the only group advocating for the legalization of some—or even all—illicit drugs.

## Marijuana Legalization

An unusual aspect of the War on Drugs has been a growing debate over whether the current approach to dealing with illegal substances should continue. Some responsible citizens, like the police officers who are members of LEAP, have questioned it. They still represent a minority of law enforcement officials, however.

Much of the attention focuses on laws against the possession of marijuana. Approximately 24 million Americans were current users of marijuana in 2016—or 8.9 percent of the population aged twelve or older. That percentage has been rising since 2002. More than 640,000 people were arrested for violating marijuana laws in 2015—89 percent of them for possession. Marijuana-related arrests comprised 43 percent of all drug arrests that year; 84 percent of arrests were for possession, a relatively low-level crime in comparison with more serious offenses such as trafficking.

Groups such as the National Organization for the Reform of Marijuana Laws (NORML) have advocated the decriminalization of marijuana use for many years. The organization also supports the right of individuals to grow marijuana plants for themselves—not to sell the drug. NORML points out that arresting violators costs federal, state, and local law enforcement agencies billions of dollars per year. Indeed, the *Lancet*, a prestigious British medical journal, has reported, "The smoking of cannabis [marijuana], even long-term, is not harmful to health. It would be reasonable to judge cannabis as less of a threat … than alcohol or tobacco."

Thirteen states have decided to decriminalize marijuana, meaning that those found in possession of small amounts of the drug are generally not prosecuted. Twenty-nine states and Washington, DC, have legalized the medical use of marijuana. In 2012, Washington and Colorado became the first US states to legalize recreational use (for personal leisure or entertainment), and seven more states have since followed suit.

Those who support changes in the marijuana laws point to legislation in Europe. Since the 1970s, the Netherlands has permitted the sale of marijuana in coffee shops in some Dutch cities. Some studies have shown that fewer adolescents smoke marijuana in the Netherlands (9.7 percent) than in England (15.8 percent), where laws are much stricter. However, the rate of marijuana use is much lower in Sweden, which has a policy of zero tolerance.

Among those opposed to liberalizing marijuana laws is the American Academy of Pediatrics. A report by the academy pointed to the effects of marijuana use. These included a negative impact on the user's concentration, attention span, short-term memory, lung function, and problem solving, which reduces an individual's ability to learn. In addition, the AAP has pointed out that someone who uses marijuana has reduced judgment and reaction time, contributing to motor-vehicle accidents and deaths among teenagers. It is especially detrimental to teenagers and children, according Dr. Seth D. Ammerman, coauthor of a 2017 AAP report: "Marijuana is not a benign drug, especially for teens. Their brains are still developing, and marijuana can cause abnormal and unhealthy changes."

The AAP has also warned that decriminalization of marijuana might result in manufacturers producing advertising designed specifically to appeal to young people. Smoking marijuana might be portrayed the way drinking has been presented—"being sexy, popular, and fun, and as an ideal means to 'break the ice' in social settings … Legalization of marijuana could decrease adolescents' perceptions of the risk of use and increase their exposure to the drug."

Experts on both sides of the debate have also discussed another issue regarding marijuana: whether it is a gateway drug, leading to the use of other, harder drugs, such as cocaine. The *Journal of the American Medical Association* has reported that young people who smoke marijuana are about two to five times more likely to use harder drugs than those who don't smoke pot. The report was based on a study of more than three hundred identical twins. One of them used marijuana while the other one did not. Half of those who smoked it moved on to more powerful drugs.

However, a 2001 report published in London, England, by the Center for Economic Policy Research based on a study of marijuana users in Amsterdam, capital of the Netherlands, "concludes that cannabis [marijuana] is not a stepping stone to using cocaine or heroin." That study included about seventeen thousand people. A study by the RAND Corporation in 2002 supported these findings.

## Medical Use of Marijuana

A lively debate is also under way about the use of marijuana for medical purposes. According to the Marijuana Policy Project, marijuana can be useful in treating pain and nausea associated with diseases such as cancer and Acquired Immune Deficiency Syndrome (AIDS). Indeed, a report issued in 1999 by the

Employee David Malpica prepares for the work day at the Takoma Wellness Center, a medical-marijuana dispensary in Washington, DC.

Institute of Medicine of the National Academy of Sciences stated that "there are some limited circumstances in which we recommend smoking marijuana for medical uses." While the federal government prohibits the use of marijuana for any purpose, twenty-nine states have ignored the federal laws and passed legislation that allows possession and sometimes cultivation of marijuana for medical use without any penalties. However, a doctor must recommend its use to a patient.

Some evidence shows that marijuana can be used to treat chronic pain and muscle stiffness related to multiple sclerosis. The drug is also sometimes used to treat epilepsy, Parkinson's disease, and other illnesses, though a meta-analysis in the *Journal of the American Medical Association* reported in 2015 that there isn't much evidence that these latter applications are effective.

# Gonzales v. Raich

In 2002, the Drug Enforcement Administration destroyed six marijuana plants being grown in California by Diane Monson—which were to be used by her and Angel Raich for medical purposes, to reduce pain and preserve their health. The marijuana use had been prescribed by a doctor. Both Raich and Monson sued the federal government, saying that their constitutional rights were being violated. Under the Constitution, the federal government can only control commerce between states, they said, and they were growing marijuana only for their own medical use in California.

The case, *Gonzalez v. Raich*, reached the US Supreme Court. The federal government argued that one violation of the Controlled Substances Act might lead to other violations in other states—affecting interstate commerce. In 2005, the Supreme Court reached a 6–3 decision. The court upheld the Controlled Substances Act, which classified marijuana as a Schedule I drug, making its use illegal in all circumstances. Writing for the majority, Justice John Paul Stevens wrote that "the regulation is squarely within Congress's commerce power." In a dissenting opinion, Justice Sandra Day O'Connor stated that federal legislation making it a crime to grow marijuana for medical purposes interfered with the rights of states to regard marijuana differently, especially when it affected the lives of state residents.

In response to the ruling, Raich—who had a wasting syndrome, among other ailments—said that marijuana was necessary for improving her appetite so she could maintain a healthy weight. She said she would keep using the drug. "I don't have a choice but to continue, because if I stopped I would die," she said.

The analysis also found that the drug can lead to some short-term adverse effects, such as dizziness, fatigue, and confusion.

In most cases, local law enforcement officials enforce the laws regarding possession. Since they follow state laws, medical use has continued regardless of federal legislation opposed to possession of marijuana. In 2005, the US Supreme Court ruled that the federal government could continue to imprison anyone who used marijuana for medical purposes. However, the Supreme Court did not throw out the state medical marijuana laws, so they continue to be in effect. A study published in 2004 by the *Journal of Drug Issues* reported that medical marijuana use had "little impact on youth and young adult marijuana-related attitudes and use." About 83 percent of Americans support the use of medical marijuana.

## Legalizing Other Drugs

The debate on legalizing the use of marijuana for medical purposes has become part of a wider discussion on whether other illicit drugs should be legalized as well. Those who support legalization argue that the War on Drugs is not effective. The Drug Enforcement Administration fights smugglers one big bust at a time, but traffickers still find other ways to bring drugs into the United States. The demand for drugs has not declined, the profits from selling them remain very high, and traffickers have been prepared to risk prison in order to keep supplying them. As police officer Peter Moskos, author of *Cop in the Hood: My Year Policing Baltimore's Eastern District*, put it, "Law enforcement can't reduce supply or demand. As a Baltimore police officer, I arrested drug dealers. Others took their place."

Ethan Nadelmann, founder of the Drug Policy Alliance, has pointed out that the United Nations declared in 1998 that its goal was "eliminating or significantly reducing the illicit cultivation of the coca bush, the cannabis plant and the opium poppy by the year 2008" and "achieving significant and measurable results in the field of demand reduction." However, none of these goals have been reached. As Nadelmann added, "global production and consumption of those drugs are roughly the same as they were a decade ago." Programs in crop eradication have been unsuccessful in cutting down demand, and some people still enjoy the feeling that comes with using drugs. None of these factors, according to Nadelmann, are likely to change.

Instead, Nadelmann added, drugs should be legalized so that they become a health issue, not a law-enforcement issue. Those who are addicted to drugs can receive treatment, even "pharmaceutical heroin from clinics." Switzerland has used this approach, and one study published in *Lancet* reported that among 7,250 patients, the number of new users declined from 850 in 1990 to 150 in 2002.

In addition, if drug use were legalized, the federal government and the states could tax its sale and potentially reduce demand. "Regulation can reduce drug use," according to Moskos. "In two generations, we've halved the number of cigarette smokers not through prohibition but through education, regulated selling, and taxes." Meanwhile, under the present system, illegal drug sales fund huge cartels in various parts of the world, and as a result, the drug trade is much more dangerous for everyone involved in it. On the other hand, in the case of marijuana, demand has increased since its legalization.

Critics of the current drug laws draw a comparison between them and the prohibition of alcohol, which became US law in 1919. The manufacture and sale of alcohol continued, however. What's more, gangsters stepped in to provide illegal alcohol to anyone who wanted to buy it. As gangs battled each other for

Sarah Denny, attending pediatric physician at the Nationwide Children's Hospital in Ohio, speaks in opposition to marijuana legalization in 2015.

control of the alcohol trade, violence broke out in cities across the United States. Finally, in 1933, Prohibition was repealed. States, however, retained laws governing where and when alcohol could be sold, preventing minors from purchasing alcohol as well as taxing it. Some experts have argued that prohibiting drugs just makes them more attractive to young people who want to experiment and defy authority or the law. Legalizing drugs, then, might reduce their attractiveness.

Nevertheless, the idea of legalizing all drugs meets with a great deal of resistance. Peter de Marneffe, a philosophy professor at Arizona State University, has argued that, since some people enjoy the high that drugs provide, drug use would rise if drugs were legalized. Marneffe added that many illicit drugs have very negative effects. "Habitual heroin use typically lowers a person's expectations of himself and decreases his concern with what others expect of him; it typically weakens a person's motivation to accomplish things and to meet his responsibilities to others."

Marneffe also wrote that the government had a responsibility to make such substances illegal. Heroin laws work to reduce the number of people who use the drug. Marneffe compared drug laws to laws against theft. Although theft has not been completely eliminated as a result of such laws, "this is no argument for their abolition." While some have argued that heroin abuse harms only the abuser and should not carry a criminal penalty, Marneffe disagreed. For example, parents who regularly use the drug are less capable of caring for their children. What's more, heroin laws "reduce the risk to young people of developing a habit that undermines their own opportunities for future achievement and well-being," he argued.

George Sher, a professor at Rice University, has pointed out that many illegal drugs also have long-term negative health effects. Regular use of cocaine and methamphetamine poses heart risks and the possibility of strokes. Like Marneffe, Sher argued that drug use harms other people besides the drug users. As he wrote in the journal *Criminal Justice Ethics*, "by drastically enhancing self-confidence, aggression and libido, these drugs elicit behavior that predictably culminates in high-speed collisions, shootouts in parking lots, and destroyed immune systems … Just as drug use can harm the user, so, too, can it harm others … Thus, one obvious reason to continue to criminalize these drugs is simply that many persons deterred by the law from using them will thereby be spared serious injury … Whatever else we say, we surely must insist that all reasonable theories of criminalization do allow governments to criminalize behavior simply on the grounds that it is too risky."

When it comes to the legalization debate, many people fall somewhere in the middle, supporting the decriminalization or even legalization of some drugs, but not all—or the legalization of drug use for specific purposes only, such as the medical use of marijuana. While the legalization of marijuana has become more and more common among American states, it has met continued resistance by federal authorities. When it comes to other illicit drugs, reduced penalties or more treatment options may be on the horizon, but legalization isn't a likely step for state or federal lawmakers to take in the foreseeable future.

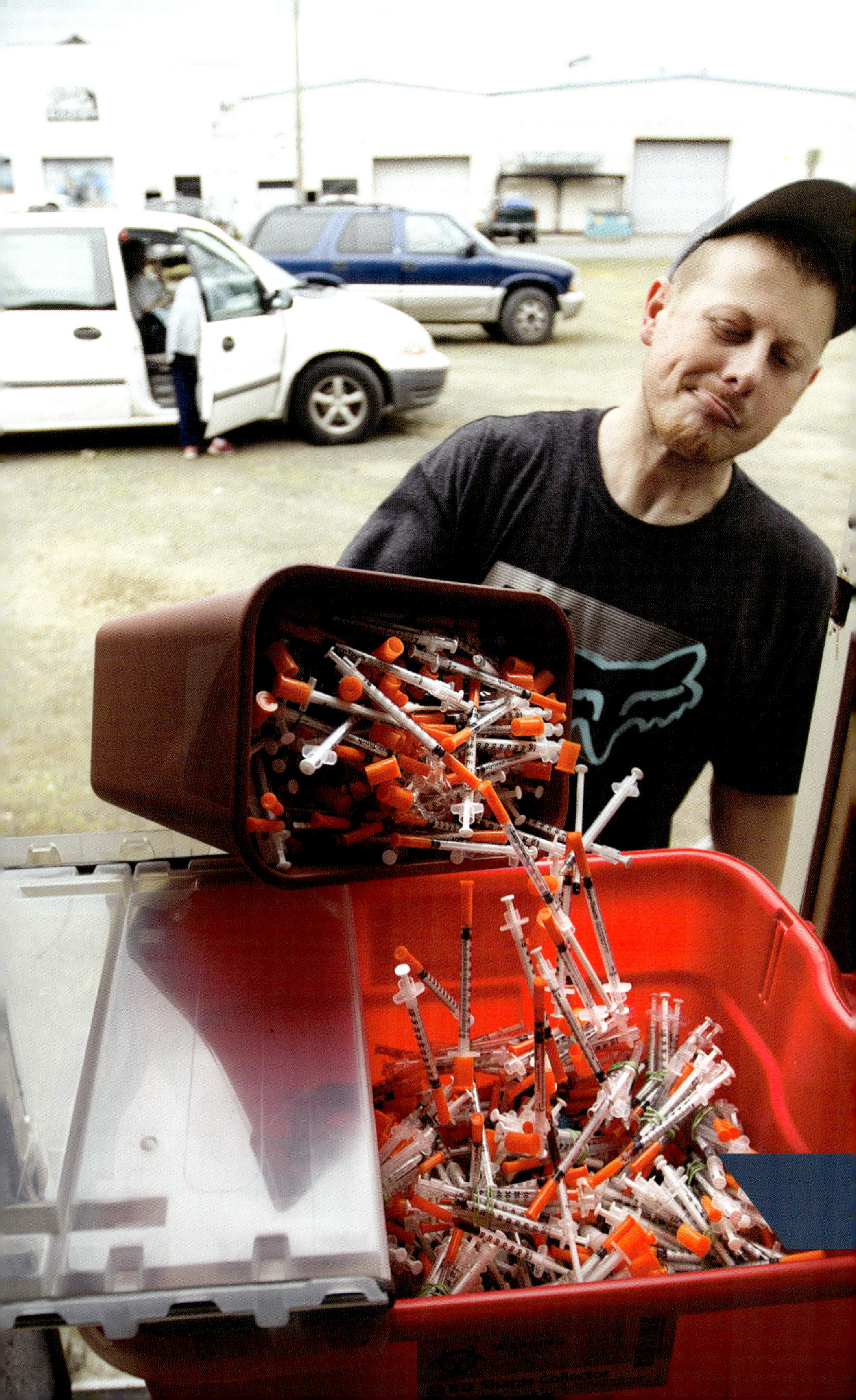

## Chapter Six

# ADDICTION TREATMENT AND HARM PREVENTION

Columbia University reports that 1.5 million American prisoners, comprising 65 percent of the prison population, are addicted to drugs. Yet only 11 percent of these individuals receive treatment for their addiction while they're incarcerated. Many argue that imprisoning drug offenders does not effectively prevent them from committing the same crime again. After all, most drug offenders are rearrested within five years of their release. Instead, some say that reducing the harm that they can cause to themselves and others and enrolling them in drug treatment programs addresses addiction as the root of the problem—and the cause of related crimes that the offender may commit, such as theft to support the purchase of drugs.

*Opposite:* Chris Burkett exchanges used needles for new ones at the Grays Harbor County Public Health and Social Services Department in Washington, which collected 750,000 needles in 2016.

# Needle-Exchange Programs

Harm reduction is an approach designed to reduce the harmful effects of drug use on addicts and those around them. Many users don't want to stop using drugs or feel that they can't stop. Advocates for harm reduction argue that, when addiction treatment fails, other measures can and should be taken to help addicts use their drug more safely.

Needle-exchange programs (also called syringe-exchange programs or needle-syringe programs) are one way to prevent addicts from suffering serious health problems. In 1984, the Dutch established a needle-exchange program in Amsterdam, capital of the Netherlands—the first of its kind anywhere in the world. The purpose of the program was to help drug addicts who were sharing needles and using them to inject heroin into their bodies. These needles were also spreading HIV, the virus that causes AIDS. Instead of reusing needles, Dutch heroin users could bring used needles to an exchange site and receive a clean needle in return. The goal was to prevent the spread of communicable diseases. The success of the Dutch program led to similar exchanges in other parts of Europe as well as in Australia. Needles became available in exchanges, pharmacies, and even vending machines. A study of the Australian program revealed that, as a result of the program, there were no new cases of HIV among intravenous drug abusers (those who used needles) over a three-year period.

Needle-exchange programs also began appearing in the United States. By 2017, thirty-nine states, Washington, DC, and Puerto Rico had a total of 299 programs. While some states had only a single program, others—such as California, New Mexico, and New York—had more than twenty. Nevertheless, needle-exchange programs have always been controversial. The US federal government, for example, has opposed these programs in the past. However, the Centers for Disease Control and Protection as well as the US Department of Health and Human Services have confirmed that syringe services programs "are an effective component of a comprehensive, integrated approach to HIV prevention." A 2016 law permitted local and state communities to use federal funds to pay for syringe services programs on a limited basis, but these funds still cannot be used to purchase needles or syringes that will be used for injecting illegal drugs.

Authors Jenny Murphy and Bryan Knowles wrote in opposition to such programs in their article "Are Needle Exchange Programs a Good Idea?" They said that "giving needles to IV [intravenous] drug addicts is like giving matches to a pyromaniac. Needle exchange programs encourage addicts to continue, or even increase, their drug use … The only way to halt the spread of disease among drug users is to halt their use of drugs."

Opponents also argue that needle-exchange programs would add to the amount of drug equipment already being used by addicts—equipment that would be financed by American tax dollars. They point to studies conducted during the 1990s in Europe, Canada, and the United States showing that needle-exchange programs had no effect on the number of AIDS cases, and in two studies even showed an increase in them. These reports have bolstered the position taken by states that have not started needle-exchange programs. In Bexar County, Texas, for example, when three members of the Bexar Area Harm Reduction Coalition began to dispense needles in 2008, they were stopped by law-enforcement officials.

However, many other studies have indicated that needle-exchange programs do work in reducing HIV and other diseases among intravenous drug users. During the late 1990s, a study by the National Institutes of Health and the Institute of Medicine revealed that HIV transmission declined by 30 percent among IV drug users as a result of needle-exchange programs. Other studies in cities such as Portland, Oregon, Tacoma, Washington, and Baltimore, Maryland, backed up these findings. Since Portugal decriminalized all drugs in 2001, the rate of HIV infection has dropped dramatically, from 104.2 new cases per million in 2000 to 4.2 new cases per million in 2015. Not all of this drop can be attributed to needle-exchange programs, given that Portugal implemented

Ashley Gardner, 34, swallows a dose of methadone at a clinic in Georgia. It's part of her treatment for opioid addiction.

a number of other measures and harm-reduction programs, but many have argued that Portugal's case stands as strong evidence for the effectiveness of harm reduction in general.

Other studies have demonstrated that needle-exchange programs do not increase intravenous drug use, as opponents of the programs fear. The Missouri Department of Health and Senior Services reported in 2004 that the programs are also cost-effective. While treating an HIV-infected child costs as much as $200,000, the cost of a needle-exchange program is only $34,278 per infection prevented.

In 2003, Vancouver, Canada, went a step further by opening "the first supervised heroin-injection clinic," according to the *Economist* magazine. Heroin addicts received clean needles, and they could also consult counselors who might help them eventually end their addictions. Then–prime minister Stephen Harper opposed the clinic because he did not believe that Canadian taxpayers should pay for people to continue their addictions. A later study showed that only a small percentage of Vancouver's addicts actually used the clinic, and that there had been no increase in addicts seeking treatment.

## Methadone Maintenance Treatment Programs

Needle exchanges are not the only controversial harm-reduction program involving drug abusers. During the 1960s, Dr. Marie Nyswander and Dr. Vincent P. Dole began working with heroin addicts at Rockefeller University in New York City. Dole had been a researcher at the university, while Nyswander was a psychiatrist who had worked at a federal hospital treating drug abusers in Lexington, Kentucky. At first, they tried to help addicts withdraw from heroin by switching them to morphine. However, as Nyswander later wrote, "on morphine the patients were rendered practically immobile. Much of the time they sat passively in front of a television set." Then the researchers tried methadone, a synthetic opium first produced in Germany during the 1930s. Surprisingly, patients on methadone became far more engaged in their lives, returned to school or work, and overcame their addiction to heroin.

At first, there was strong opposition to the use of methadone as a substitute for heroin. Many experts who supported a zero-tolerance approach to drugs believed that methadone simply replaced one drug addiction with another. Nevertheless, the early studies proved very promising. One study of over five hundred addicts in New York City during the late 1960s demonstrated that within "three months of starting methadone maintenance, more than half of the male addicts were productively employed or attending school. After a year the proportion rose to two-thirds." In addition to providing participants with methadone, the study also included psychological counseling from trained personnel.

Methadone is an artificial opiate that acts as a blocker against the high associated with heroin. It also reduces the desire for the drug as well as the difficult physical effects of withdrawal. However, methadone did not ultimately deliver the cure for the heroin problem that some researchers were hoping for. As methadone programs increased, some of them did not provide patients with a high enough dosage of methadone to be effective. In addition, many heroin addicts did not join the program, or did not stay with the program long enough for it to be effective. Currently, there is still opposition to methadone programs by those who believe in zero drug tolerance. Still, there are nearly sixteen hundred medication-assisted opioid treatment clinics in the United States. (Methadone is also prescribed by doctors as a painkiller. Some patients, however, have died from the drug after receiving too strong a dosage.)

According to the National Institute on Drug Abuse, a federal agency that conducts research into drug abuse, "for methadone maintenance, 12 months of treatment is the minimum, and some opiate-addicted individuals will continue to benefit from methadone maintenance treatment over a period of years." Studies have shown that the programs can be very effective for those who continue treatment long enough, and who receive substantial doses of methadone. In three months, only about 10 percent of these patients continued using heroin. Criminal activity among patients was also reduced. After a patient has transitioned from heroin to methadone, the dosage is then—in many cases—gradually reduced. This helps the person avoid some of the most severe withdrawal symptoms, which can include muscle aches, anxiety, and nausea.

For methadone maintenance treatment to be effective, patients also need counseling, because methadone does not totally eliminate the desire for heroin or provide patients with the skills to resist their cravings for the drug.

Unfortunately, many patients don't want to give up heroin. Some enter a methadone program but leave too early and return to heroin addiction. Others continue using heroin even while attending the program, while still others sell the methadone and make a profit to finance their heroin addiction. This is an indication of how difficult many addicts find the task of ending their addiction. Similar problems occur among alcoholics who try to give up drinking. Even heavy cigarette smokers have discovered that giving up their smoking habit can be extremely difficult.

The mixed results of methadone and other drug substitution programs may partly account for the opposition that still exists to using the drugs. A PBS report by journalist Bill Moyers noted that "misconceptions abound and continue to limit methadone's availability. Neighborhood groups often oppose a new clinic

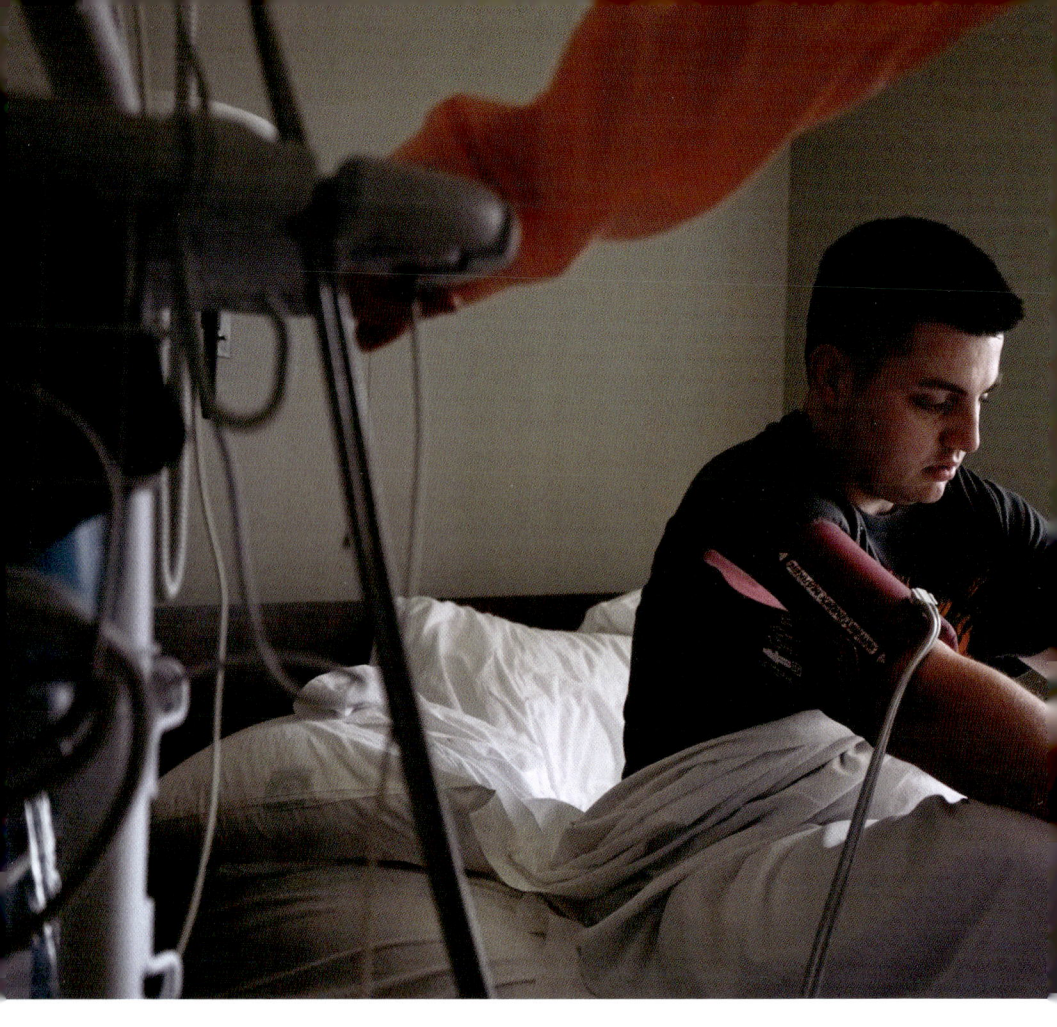

Recovering heroin addict Stephen Barbour receives treatment in a residential treatment facility in Massachusetts in 2016.

because they assume it will lead to higher rates of drug use and crime [studies show these rates actually go down]." In addition, drug laws generally require patients to come to a methadone clinic daily to receive their dosage of the drug. This may be inconvenient for some people who hold down steady jobs, so they stop attending the program. However, some longtime patients now receive permission to receive as much as a four-week supply of the drug to take at home, making the methadone program easier. Tens of thousands of Americans take methadone to fight addiction, and these programs are far cheaper than putting a heroin addict in prison.

## Addiction Treatment

Treatment programs for drug abuse have often been controversial because of society's attitudes toward addiction. For centuries, drug addicts were generally considered to be weak or bad people who lacked the desire or strength to change their lives. These attitudes have been slow to change. While the initial decision to use drugs may be voluntary, scientists now realize that drug use can produce a lasting impact on the brain. Illicit drugs such as heroin raise the level of a brain chemical called dopamine, which affects a person's ability to experience pleasure and pain. Over time, as a person continues to take a drug, the brain requires more and more of it to be satisfied and experience pleasure, according to a 2004 report to Congress by Dr. Nora Volkow, director of the National Institute on Drug Abuse.

As a result, "judgment and decision-making circuits become impaired, and the individual's overriding motivation becomes seeking and taking drugs."

Volkow explained that drug addiction is much like other chronic illnesses, such as heart disease and cancer. "Like these other chronic diseases, drug addiction can be effectively treated and managed over its course, but this requires treatments to be readily available and adhered to." Unfortunately, addicts, like some of those who suffer from heart disease or diabetes, don't always follow the required treatments. In fact, studies indicate that only one-half of patients with diabetes or heart disease take their medications and follow the treatments prescribed by their

# Drug Abuse Prevention

Drug use can begin early—even in childhood or adolescence. In such cases, the National Institute on Drug Abuse regards it as a developmental disorder that can grow worse and lead to addiction as a child grows older. As a result, the institute has urged doctors to

*Personnel from Grissom Air Reserve Base guide Indiana schoolchildren through an exercise on how to resist peer pressure.*

become more aware of young patients who may have a drug problem and help them find treatment.

Many schools have also initiated drug-prevention programs to stop drug abuse before it can begin. Among these are LifeSkills Training, which is aimed at children in elementary school and middle school. The program helps young people make decisions, deal with stress, and resist peer pressure to use drugs. Another program, called Project ALERT, is aimed at middle-school students. This program led to a decline in marijuana use by as much as 60 percent. The Project ALERT program includes several lessons taught weekly that help students deal with the peer pressure they might encounter to use drugs such as marijuana. It also emphasizes the reasons not to begin using drugs.

A third program is Drug Abuse Resistance Education, or DARE. Started in the 1980s, the program was taught by uniformed police officers and used by schools throughout the United States and in Canada. However, decades of research concluded that DARE was not effective in keeping kids off drugs. So in 2009, DARE changed its mission to become less drug-focused, and to instead "teach students good decision making skills to help them lead safe and healthy lives." It also began implementing more strategies that evidence has proven to work.

Addiction Treatment and Harm Prevention

doctors. It comes as no surprise, then, that drug users might follow a similar pattern.

Volkow also pointed out that effective drug treatment involves a "continuum of care." This includes counseling to help those who are trying to quit using drugs or trying to remain sober after having quit. Counseling with former cocaine addicts, for example, enables them to discuss the negative impact of using cocaine again. The counseling also helps patients understand the situations they are likely to encounter in which they might be tempted to begin using cocaine and how to cope with these situations effectively. Other types of counseling help patients avoid situations where they might be tempted to use drugs and change the thoughts or feelings that might lead to drug use.

For example, in the 1980s, Delaware established a program involving counseling that was aimed at helping convicted drug users. This program, which is still under way, decreases drug use and keeps former abusers from returning to prison. The first part of the program begins while offenders are still in prison. About a year and a half before their release, recovering drug abusers, who live in a separate part of the prison community, receive extensive counseling every day. The second part of the program places offenders in a special work-release program. Participants continue to receive counseling as well as help finding jobs in the community. During this time, they are employed each day at a job and return to the center at night. In the final component of the program, offenders released from prison work at their jobs and live with families in the community. They continue counseling at the prison center and are regularly tested for drug use.

Studies of the program have demonstrated that more than three quarters of those who completed all three parts stopped using drugs. More than 70 percent were not arrested again. Surveys of treatment programs in other states by the National

Association of State Alcohol and Drug Abuse Directors Inc. have also indicated that the longer individuals stay in treatment, the better their outcome is likely to be. Those who stayed in the Delaware program were far more likely to remain drug-free six months after the treatment was completed. They also held down jobs, and the crime rate among them was greatly reduced. Indeed, one study indicated that a dollar spent on drug treatment led to as much as seven dollars saved because of the reduction in crime. Aftercare (treatment after prison) also makes a big difference in the rate of success. In addition, many people have benefited from support groups, such as Narcotics Anonymous.

Other approaches to drug-addiction treatment include long-term stays at residential care facilities—often for six to twelve months—and short-term stays of three to six weeks incorporating a twelve-step approach similar to that used in Alcoholics Anonymous. These programs often help users through the detoxification process, during which the drugs leave their system and addicts often suffer difficult side effects. Group counseling with organizations such as Narcotics Anonymous can also be effective.

4th Amendment

## Chapter Seven

# DRUGS AND CONSTITUTIONAL RIGHTS

Some have alleged that the War on Drugs has led to widespread and repeated violations of Americans' constitutional rights—in particular, their right to privacy and protection from unreasonable searches. Several pivotal legal cases have weighed in on what types of investigations or searches are permissible under the US Constitution.

## Drugs in Schools

A number of US Supreme Court cases have been pivotal in determining when and whether searches, seizures, and drug tests should be permissible in public schools.

*Opposite:* The Fourth Amendment to the US Constitution protects Americans from unreasonable searches.

## New Jersey v. TLO

In 1980, two teenage girls stood inside the principal's office at Piscataway High School in New Jersey. This was the beginning of a legal case that eventually reached the US Supreme Court. The girls, whose names were withheld because of their age, were accused of smoking cigarettes in the bathroom, a violation of school rules. Although one of the girls said she had been smoking, the other one denied it. When her purse was searched, however, it contained cigarettes as well as something else: marijuana, along with information indicating that the girl was selling the drug to her classmates. When the girl was taken into custody by police, she admitted to dealing drugs and received a sentence of one year's probation by a state court. However, the sentence was revoked by the New Jersey Supreme Court, which said that her constitutional rights under the Fourth Amendment had been violated.

The state supreme court ruled that, when the purse of the young girl at Piscataway High School was searched without a warrant, it was a violation of her Fourth-Amendment rights. However, the New Jersey attorney general—the highest legal officer in the state—was not convinced and appealed the decision to the US Supreme Court.

The case, known as *New Jersey v. TLO*, reached the Supreme Court in 1984. Since the girl was less than eighteen years old—a minor—her name was withheld and only her initials were used. The state of New Jersey argued that, because of the girl's suspicious behavior, high school officials were within their rights when they searched her purse without a warrant. School officials should have powers to control student behavior while in school, they argued—just as parents control the behavior of their children at home.

The lawyers for TLO took a different position, pointing out that school officials are not parents and insisting that their client's rights under the Fourth Amendment had indeed been

# The Fourth Amendment

The Fourth Amendment is part of the Bill of Rights, which is designed to ensure specific rights and freedoms and limit the power of the US government. The Bill of Rights comprises the first ten amendments to the United States Constitution and was ratified on December 15, 1791.

The Fourth Amendment to the US Constitution states:

> The right of the people to be secure in their persons, houses, papers, and effects, against unreasonable searches and seizures, shall not be violated, and no Warrants shall issue, but upon probable cause, supported by Oath or affirmation, and particularly describing the place to be searched, and the persons or things to be seized.

Courts enforce the Fourth Amendment in part through the exclusionary rule, by which evidence collected in violation of the amendment cannot generally be admitted legally as evidence in a court of law. This means that if a law-enforcement official makes a search without reasonable suspicion or without a warrant—even if he or she finds evidence of illegal activity during that search—whatever is found cannot be held against a defendant in a criminal trial.

violated. According to the exclusionary rule, which is based on constitutional law, evidence obtained by an illegal seizure could not be used in a court of law and, therefore, TLO's conviction should be overturned.

In its consideration of the case, the Supreme Court sought to balance a student's right to privacy against the "interest of teachers and administrators in maintaining discipline in the classroom and on school grounds. Maintaining order in the classroom has never been easy," read the court's majority opinion, penned by Justice Byron White. "But in recent years, school disorder has often taken particularly ugly forms: drug use and violent crime in the schools have become major social problems."

In an earlier case, the Supreme Court had permitted police officers to stop and search a suspect if there was reasonable suspicion that the suspect had committed a crime. Since the police had to act quickly, and there was no time to obtain a warrant from a judge, they could conduct the search without a warrant. Justice White added that the same principles applied to school settings because it "would unduly interfere with the maintenance of the swift and informal disciplinary procedures needed in schools."

Furthermore, the court ruled that schools did not have to comply with the standard of probable cause to conduct a search. They could use a more flexible standard: "reasonableness," which is not as strong as "probable." This standard was necessary for school officials to do their job effectively, the court concluded. In the case of TLO, school officials had "reasonable grounds" or reasonable suspicion—although they could not be certain that it was probable—for believing that the girl was violating school policy and smoking in the bathroom. This led to a search of her purse and the discovery of the cigarettes and the marijuana.

The Supreme Court ruled in favor of the state of New Jersey by a vote of 6–3. As the majority opinion of Justice White put it, "we reaffirmed that the constitutional rights of students in public school are not automatically coextensive with the rights of adults in other settings."

## *Vernonia School District v. Acton*

In 1995, the Supreme Court reached a similar decision in another case regarding drug policies in schools. This case involved a student athlete named James Acton who refused to take a drug test at his school in Vernonia, Oregon. The school district had instituted a policy of testing athletes for drugs. The urinalysis tests occurred at the start of the school year and at random times during the athletic season. School officials had begun the program because an increasing number of students were causing disciplinary problems. School officials believed that these problems were linked to drugs. Among those most involved in the school district's drug culture were student athletes. Coaches were concerned that the use of drugs had led to the severe injury of a wrestler and might affect other athletes as well. At first, the school district had attempted to deal with the problem by initiating a drug-education program. When this did not work, Vernonia officials—with approval of the school district's parents—turned to the drug-testing policy.

Acton refused to be tested, arguing that it was an invasion of his privacy protected by the Fourth Amendment. He said that there was no reasonable cause for the school to assume that he was using drugs. The Supreme Court, however, ultimately disagreed in a 6–3 decision handed down by Justice Antonin Scalia. In the case of *Vernonia School District v. Acton*, referring to the court's decision in the TLO case, Scalia said that a "proper educational environment requires close supervision of school children, as well as the enforcement of rules against conduct that would be perfectly permissible if undertaken by an adult." The court added that schoolchildren "are routinely required to submit to various physical examinations and to be vaccinated

James Acton (*third from left*) leaves the Supreme Court on March 28, 1995, after a hearing in *Vernonia School District v. Acton*.

against various diseases." Student athletes are also required to take a physical exam before being permitted to play on a team. Thus schoolchildren, especially student athletes, "have a lesser expectation of privacy." The court added that an athlete's privacy was not violated by a urinalysis.

Finally, Justice Scalia stated, "Deterring drug use by our Nation's school children is at least as important as enhancing efficient enforcement of the Nation's laws against the importation of drugs." In addition, since the athletes were "role models" for other students and drug use might be "of particular danger to athletes," Justice Scalia believed that Vernonia School District should have the right to enforce a drug-testing program.

Several justices on the Supreme Court, however, disagreed. Justice Sandra Day O'Connor, joined by Justices John Paul Stevens and David Souter in a dissenting opinion, pointed out that the Fourth Amendment regards a "blanket search" of people—regardless of whether they are under suspicion of committing a crime—as unreasonable. Therefore, drug testing all student athletes—whether or not they were suspected of taking drugs—was an unreasonable intrusion on their privacy under the Fourth Amendment. O'Connor added that school officials had substantial evidence that some students were using drugs and, therefore, the testing should have been limited only to them.

## *Board of Education v. Earls*

The controversy surrounding the *Vernonia v. Acton* decision resurfaced in 2002, when the Supreme Court handed down a 5–4 ruling against a student named Lindsay Earls. In this case, which was called *Board of Education v. Earls*, the Tecumseh, Oklahoma, school district had initiated a testing policy for students participating in extracurricular activities to counter an increase in drug use among students. Earls was a member of the marching band and the choir who said that testing was a violation of her Fourth Amendment rights because there was no reason to suspect that she had used drugs.

In delivering the majority decision, Justice Clarence Thomas stated that a "student's privacy interest is limited in a public school environment where the State is responsible for maintaining discipline, health and safety." He found that drug testing was a negligible intrusion on a student's privacy and that "the only consequence of a failed drug test is to limit the student's privilege of participating in extracurricular activities."

But Justice Ruth Bader Ginsburg disagreed. Ginsburg was joined in her dissenting opinion by Justices Sandra Day O'Connor, John Paul Stevens, and David Souter. Ginsburg felt that the policy "targets for testing a student population least likely to be at risk from illicit drugs and their damaging effects." She added that the case was far different from the facts in the Vernonia School District decision. The dissenters agreed that "students who participate in extracurricular activities are significantly less likely to develop substance abuse problems than their less-involved peers."

# Defining Illegal Search

In school-related cases like those summarized above, the Supreme Court ruled that different interpretations of the law apply to schoolchildren than to adults. Defining how the Fourth Amendment should be applied in cases where adults have been involved has presented its own set of challenges.

Since the War on Drugs began, the number of controversial cases involving the Fourth Amendment has increased. They not only involve students in school settings, but adults in the community. During the 1960s, the Supreme Court ruled that a police officer who has reasonable suspicion that someone is doing something illegal has the right to stop and question that person and even look for a gun without a warrant. However, in the 1993 case *Minnesota v. Dickerson*, the court ruled that the police cannot go much further. When the police stopped Timothy Dickerson, he had been seen leaving a crack house, and they thought he might be a drug trafficker. Dickerson was stopped and searched for a gun, but none was found. However, the police did feel something in Dickerson's pocket and took out a package of cocaine. The Supreme Court ruled that the police had gone too far. They had no reason to think that the package was cocaine. Only after they removed it did they know it was an illegal drug. Therefore, Dickerson could not be convicted on the evidence discovered by the police.

Clearly, the meaning of reasonable suspicion may be difficult to define. In 1989, for example, the court looked at a number of factors and decided that they all added up to reasonable suspicion in the case of *United States v. Sokolow*. The case involved Andrew Sokolow, who in 1984 used an assumed name to purchase round-trip airline tickets from Hawaii to Miami. To pay for them, he pulled out a large roll of cash. The ticket agent was surprised that Sokolow was carrying so much cash, rather than a credit card. The agent also thought that Sokolow "appeared nervous" and contacted local police. The police conducted an investigation and discovered that Sokolow was returning from Miami after a short visit and stopping off at other cities en route to a return to Hawaii. The Drug Enforcement Administration (DEA) was brought into the case and their agents followed Sokolow on one of his stops, finally arresting him when he returned to Hawaii. With the help of a drug-sniffing dog, the DEA discovered drugs in one of Sokolow's bags. After obtaining a warrant, they searched the rest of his luggage and found evidence that he was a drug trafficker. The search of another bag turned up a large quantity of cocaine.

Sokolow claimed that the search of his bags had violated his rights under the Fourth Amendment. A lower court stated that the DEA agents had reasonable suspicion to believe that Sokolow

Christian Peralta, a detective with the Broward Sheriff's Office in Florida, searches a stolen car for drugs in 2015. He's particularly on the lookout for Flakka, a highly dangerous synthetic drug.

was involved in drug trafficking. The Supreme Court agreed in a 7–2 decision, concluding that reasonable suspicion does not need to be as strict as probable cause and can be enough to convict a suspected drug dealer. In this case, the court used the suspicious actions of the suspect—using a large roll of bills, booking tickets under an assumed name, and frequent stopovers—as a profile of common behaviors that seemed typical of other drug traffickers.

Two justices on the court, however, disagreed. Justices William Brennan and Thurgood Marshall dissented in the case, pointing out that Sokolow had not committed any illegal acts while making his travel arrangements. They also added that perfectly innocent passengers become nervous when taking airplane flights, and that nervousness is therefore no reason to alert police or suspect someone of a crime.

The court's interpretation of the Fourth Amendment has often led to strong disagreements among the justices. In 2001, the court considered the case of *Kyllo v. United States*. Using a special technology called thermal (heat) imaging, a federal agent had discovered that a high level of heat was coming from Danny Lee Kyllo's home in Oregon. The agent suspected that Kyllo was using artificial lights to grow marijuana plants inside his house. Based on this suspicion, the agent obtained a search warrant, and one hundred plants were discovered inside Kyllo's home.

Kyllo claimed that the use of the device by the federal agent was an illegal search, prohibited under the Fourth Amendment. The Supreme Court agreed. In a 5–4 decision, Justice Antonin Scalia said that thermal imaging qualified as an illegal search because no warrant had been obtained. Therefore, it was illegal under the Fourth Amendment, which protects an individual's home from a warrantless search. However, Justice John Paul Stevens disagreed. He stated that excessive heat from Kyllo's home could have been detected even without a thermal-imaging device. The agent could have simply stood near the house and felt the heat. Therefore, it was not a search of Kyllo's home, no warrant was necessary for the imaging, and the agent's actions were not illegal under the Fourth Amendment.

Although the Supreme Court has protected the home of a suspect from a search without a warrant, it has taken a different position on automobiles. If police suspect that drugs are being carried in an automobile, they can stop and search without a warrant.

## Fighting Back Against Drug Abuse

In dealing with drug abuse, there are no easy answers. Respected jurists sitting on the Supreme Court disagree over how the US Constitution should be interpreted in cases involving the use and sale of illegal drugs. Public officials and medical experts take different sides over the kinds of treatment that should be made available to drug users, or whether certain types of illicit drugs should be legalized. They also hold diverse views over the effectiveness or the future course of the War on Drugs.

Whatever the best solution or solutions may be, the use and abuse of illicit drugs remains a serious problem in the United States. Tens of thousands of people die each year from drug overdoses, and millions use cocaine, heroin, and other dangerous and addictive drugs. Finding the best way to protect individuals, families, and communities from the harm these drugs can cause will be a collaborative effort.

# Glossary

**cannabis** The plant from which marijuana is derived.

**cartel** A group of businesses united for commercial advantage.

**cocaine** An addictive drug derived from coca leaves.

**coextensive** Occupying the same space; the same as.

**decriminalization** The act of removing or lessening the criminal classification of or typical punishment for a crime.

**defendant** A person or group against whom a civil or criminal case is brought.

**disparities** Differences.

**epidemic** An outbreak of sudden rapid growth, spread, or development.

**gateway drug** A drug whose use is believed to lead to the use of harder drugs.

**heroin** An addictive drug derived from the opium poppy.

**illicit** Illegal; not permitted.

**incarceration** Confinement in a prison or jail.

**lucrative** Profitable.

**marijuana** A drug derived from the dried leaves of the cannabis plant; also called "weed" or "pot."

**methamphetamine** An addictive drug made from a variety of chemicals, including acetone (used in nail-polish remover and paint thinner), lithium (used in batteries), toluene (used in brake fluid), pseudoephedrine, and sulfuric acid.

**misconception** An inaccurate idea or belief.

**narcotic** A drug that relieves pain, induces sleep, or dulls the senses in moderate doses.

**opioid** A highly addictive class of drugs used for pain relief that can either be legally prescribed by a doctor or sold and used illegally under the common name "heroin."

**parole** The conditional release of a prisoner during which time that prisoner's behavior is monitored.

**scourge** A cause of widespread or great pain, distress, or suffering.

**stimulant** A type of drug that makes the body or parts of the body temporarily more active.

**warrant** A document giving a law-enforcement office permission to make an arrest, a seizure, or a search.

**withdrawal** In this case, the discontinuance of drug use, and the often painful physical and psychological symptoms experienced during this process.

# Further Information

## Books

Edelfield, Bruce, and Tracey J. Moosa. *Drug Abuse.* Teen Mental Health. New York: Rosen Publishing Group, 2011.

Kuhar, Michael. *The Addicted Brain: Why We Abuse Drugs, Alcohol, and Nicotine.* Upper Saddle River, NJ: Pearson Education, 2014.

Kuhn, Cynthia, Scott Swartzwelder, and Wilkie Wilson. *Buzzed: The Straight Facts About the Most Used and Abused Drugs from Alcohol to Ecstasy.* New York: W. W. Norton & Company: 2014.

Sheff, Nic. *We All Fall Down: Living with Addiction.* New York, NY. Hachette Book Group: 2012.

## Websites

**Bureau of Justice Statistics: Drug and Crime Facts**
https://www.bjs.gov/content/dcf/enforce.cfm

This site compiles key data regarding drug-related arrests and seizures, broken down by demographics and time periods, in the United States.

**National Institute on Drug Abuse**
http://www.drugabuse.gov

This website shares basic information on different drugs of abuse, key facts about drug use and addiction in the United States, and links to research briefs.

**Substance Abuse and Mental Health Services Administration**
https://www.samhsa.gov

Learn about drug use and its ties with the criminal justice system and the spread of disease on this repository of useful drug-related data.

## Videos

**Anyone Can Become Addicted to Drugs**
https://www.youtube.com/watch?v=SY2luGTX7Dk

This video from the National Institute on Drug Abuse explains the dangers of drug addiction and just how easy it can be to become addicted.

**The Heroin-Ravaged City Fighting Back Against Drug Companies**
http://www.bbc.com/news/av/world-us-canada-39343289/the-heroin-ravaged-city-fighting-back

This video features the mayor and law-enforcement officers in Huntington, West Virginia, about the opioid epidemic there and what the city is doing to fight back. The video contains some disturbing scenes of drug use.

**How Drug Addiction Works**
https://www.youtube.com/watch?v=rJSDgvWQSYI

What happens in the brain when a person becomes addicted to a drug? This animated video explains how addiction transforms the brain.

## Organizations

**Canadian Drug Policy Coalition**
Simon Fraser University #2400
515 West Hastings Street
Vancouver, BC V6B 5K3
(778) 782-5148

http://drugpolicy.ca

This group of seventy organizations and three thousand individuals supports science-based drug policy in Canada.

**Center for the Study and Prevention of Violence**
Institute of Behavioral Science
1440 15th Street
Boulder, CO 80302
(303) 492-1032
https://www.colorado.edu/cspv/mission.html

This organization conducts research to support and implement evidence-based programs and policies leading to the positive development of young people and reducing problem behaviors such as substance abuse.

**Centre for Addiction and Mental Health**
1001 Queen St. W
Toronto, ON
M6J 1H4
(800) 463-6273
http://www.camh.ca

Canada's largest addiction teaching and mental health hospital offers up key research and information about programs and services related to drug use and addiction.

**Drug Enforcement Administration**
800 K Street, NW, Suite 500
Washington, DC 20001
(202) 305-8500
https://www.dea.gov

This governmental organization seeks to enforce the drug laws of the United States and prevent the illegal trafficking and use of dangerous substances.

**Drug Policy Alliance**
131 West 33rd Street, 15th Floor
New York, New York 10001
(212) 613-8020
http://www.drugpolicy.org

The Drug Policy Alliance works to promote policies that reduce the harms associated with drug use and prohibition. It promotes drug-regulatory policies based on science, health, and human rights.

**National Drug Court Institute**
625 N. Washington, Ste. 212
Alexandria, VA 22314
(703) 575-9400
https://www.ndci.org

Formed in 1997, the National Drug Court Institute promotes evidence-based training and assistance to drug courts throughout the United States.

# Bibliography

"About Marijuana." National Organization for the Reform of Marijuana Laws (NORML), June 28, 2008. http://norml.org/marijuana.

"Alcohol and Other Drug Treatment Effectiveness: A Review of State Outcome Studies." National Association of State Alcohol and Drug Abuse Directors, 2008. http://www.nasadad.org/index.php?doc_id=91.

American Academy of Pediatrics, Committee on Substance Abuse and Committee on Adolescence. "Legalization of Marijuana: Potential Impact on Youth." *Pediatrics* 113, no. 6 (June 2004): 1825–1826.

Associated Press. "More West Virginia Towns, Counties Sue over Opioid Crisis." *US News*, March 15, 2018. https://www.usnews.com/news/best-states/west-virginia/articles/2018-03-15/2-more-west-virginia-counties-sue-over-opioid-crisis.

——————. "West Virginia to Depose Top Pharma Execs in Opioid Lawsuit." *Seattle Times*, March 6, 2018. https://www.seattletimes.com/nation-world/west-virginia-to-depose-top-pharma-execs-in-opioid-lawsuit.

Azami, Dawood. "Why Afghanistan May Never Eradicate Opium." BBC World Service, February 26, 2013. http://www.bbc.com/news/world-asia-21548230.

Blake, Andrew. "Americans Overwhelmingly Favor Medical Marijuana, Split on Recreational Weed: Poll." *Washington Times*, April 18, 2017. https://www.washingtontimes.com/news/2017/apr/18/83-percent-americans-favor-legalizing-medical-weed.----

Blau, Max. "Stat Forecast: Opioids Could Kill Nearly 500,000 Americans in the Next Decade." *STAT*, June 27, 2017. https://www.statnews.com/2017/06/27/opioid-deaths-forecast.

———. "'This Is Just the Beginning': Scope of Opioid Lawsuits Widens to Include Hospital Accreditor." *STAT*, November 7, 2017. https://www.statnews.com/2017/11/07/opioid-lawsuit-hospital-accreditor.

Booth, Martin. *Cannabis, A History*. New York: St. Martin's Press, 2003.

"BOP Drug Treatment Programs Work: Treatment of Inmates' Addictions to Drugs (TRIAD)." Federal Bureau of Prisons, May 1, 2012. https://www.bop.gov/resources/pdfs/triad_summary050112.pdf.

Borchardt, Debra. "Report: Total Marijuana Demand Tops Ice Cream in U.S." *Forbes*, May 17, 2017. https://www.forbes.com/sites/debraborchardt/2017/05/17/new-report-says-total-marijuana-demand-tops-ice-cream/#32b7291a5b5e.

Boundy, Donna. "Profile: Methadone Maintenance, The 'Invisible' Success Story." *Moyers on Addiction: Close to Home*. Thirteen/WNET. Accessed December 12, 2008. http://www.pbs.org/wnet/closetohome/treatment/html/methprofile.html.

Butterfield, Fox. "Decline of Violent Crimes Is Linked to Crack Market." *New York Times,* December 28, 1998. https://www.nytimes.com/1998/12/28/us/decline-of-violent-crimes-is-linked-to-crack-market.html.

Bureau of Justice Statistics, "Drug Law Violations: Enforcement." US Department of Justice. Accessed December 12, 2008. http://www.ojp.usdoj.gov/bjs/dcf/enforce.htm.

Carroll, Lauren. "How the War on Drugs Affected Incarceration Rates." *PolitiFact,* July 10, 2016. http://www.politifact.com/truth-o-meter/statements/2016/jul/10/cory-booker/how-war-drugs-affected-incarceration-rates.

Center for the Study and Prevention of Violence. "Blueprints Promising Programs: Project ALERT." Institute of Behavioral Science, University of Colorado at Boulder, 2006. http://www.colorado.edu/cspv/publications/fact-sheets/blueprints/FS-BPP13.pdf.

Chang, Ailsa. "Lawyer Behind West Virginia County Lawsuit Against Opioid Distributors." NPR, April 20, 2017. https://www.npr.org/2017/04/20/524936058/lawyer-behind-west-virginia-county-lawsuit-against-opioid-distributors.

CNN Wire. "18-Ton Cocaine Bust Displayed at San Diego Pier by US Coast Guard." WTKR, June 17, 2017. http://wtkr.com/2017/06/16/18-ton-cocaine-bust-displayed-at-san-diego-pier-by-us-coast-guard.

Corr, Anders. "To Defeat Terrorism in Afghanistan, Start with Opium Crops in Nangarhar Province." *Forbes*, March 26, 2017. https://

www.forbes.com/sites/anderscorr/2017/03/26/to-defeat-terrorism-in-afghanistan-start-with-opium-crops-in-nangarhar-province/#48c8199e57d3.

Davis, Tom, Mark E. Souder, and Charles E. Grassley, "Drug Control: Air Bridge Denial Program in Colombia Has Implemented New Safeguards, but Its Effect on Drug Trafficking Is Not Clear." Government Accountability Office, report to congressional requesters, September 2005. http://www.gao.gov/new.items/d05970.pdf.

"DEA Programs: Cannabis Eradication." Drug Enforcement Administration. Accessed March 29, 2018. https://www.dea.gov/ops/cannabis.shtml.

"DEA Programs: Money Laundering." Drug Enforcement Administration. Accessed March 30, 2018. https://www.dea.gov/ops/money.shtml.

"DEA Task Force Eradicates $20 Million Marijuana Grown in CA National Forest." US Drug Enforcement Administration, July 14, 2008. http://www.justice.gov/dea/pubs/states/newsrel/sd071408.html.

"Debunking the 'Gateway' Myth." Drug Policy Alliance, February 2017. https://www.drugpolicy.org/sites/default/files/DebunkingGatewayMyth_NY_0.pdf.

"Decision and Rationale," *New Jersey v. T.L.O.* (1985). http://www.infoplease.com/us/supreme-court/cases/ar24.html.

De Marneffe, Peter. "Against the Legalization of Heroin." *Criminal Justice Ethics,* Winter/Spring 2003.

Eckholm, Erik. "Innovative Courts Give Some Addicts Chance to Straighten Out." *New York Times,* October 15, 2008. https://www.nytimes.com/2008/10/15/us/15drugs.html.

"The Federal Drug Control Budget." Drug Policy Alliance, February 2015. https://www.drugpolicy.org/sites/default/files/DPA_Fact_sheet_Drug_War_Budget_Feb2015.pdf.

Ferreira, Susana. "Portugal's Radical Drugs Policy Is Working. Why Hasn't the World Copied It?" *Guardian*, December 5, 2017. https://www.theguardian.com/news/2017/dec/05/portugals-radical-drugs-policy-is-working-why-hasnt-the-world-copied-it.

Friedman, Thomas L. "Drilling in Afghanistan." *New York Times,* July 30, 2008. https://www.nytimes.com/2008/07/30/opinion/30friedman.html.

Gray, James P. *Why Our Drug Laws Have Failed and What We Can Do About It.* Philadelphia, PA: Temple University Press, 2001.

Greenhouse, Linda. "Justices Uphold Federal Medical-Marijuana Prosecutions." *New York Times*, June 5, 2005. https://www.nytimes.com/2005/06/06/politics/justices-uphold-federal-medicalmarijuana-prosecutions.html.

Guy, Gery P. Jr., Kun Zhang, Michele K. Bohm, et al. "Vital Signs: Changes in Opioid Prescribing in the United States, 2006–2015." *Morbidity and Mortality Weekly Report* 66, no. 26 (July 7, 2017): 697–704. http://dx.doi.org/10.15585/mmwr.mm6626a4.

Hamilton, Keegan. "Opioid Overload: Drug Companies Sued for Flooding West Virginia County with 40 Million Doses of Opioids." *VICE News*, March 10, 2017. https://news.vice.com/en_us/article/mb9yby/drug-companies-sued-for-flooding-west-virginia-county-with-40-million-doses-of-opioids.

Higham, Scott, and Lenny Bernstein. "The Drug Industry's Triumph over the DEA." *Washington Post,* October 15, 2017. https://www.washingtonpost.com/graphics/2017/investigations/dea-drug-industry-congress/https://www.washingtonpost.com/graphics/2017/investigations/dea-drug-industry-congress/?utm_term=.256ea99ca898.

Holstege, Sean. "Huge Heroin Bust a Sign of Drug's Return," *Arizona Republic*, July 11, 2008. http://archive.azcentral.com/arizonarepublic/news/articles/2008/07/11/20080711heroin0711.html.

Huddleston, C. West, III. "Drug Courts: An Effective Strategy for Communities Facing Methamphetamine." US Department of Justice, Office of Justice Assistance, May 2005.

Humphreys, Keith. "Americans Use Far More Opioids Than Anyone Else in the World." *Washington Post*, March 15, 2017. https://www.washingtonpost.com/news/wonk/wp/2017/03/15/americans-use-far-more-opioids-than-anyone-else-in-the-world/?utm_term=.888052727283.

Ingraham, Christopher. "A Brief History of DARE, the Anti-Drug Program Jeff Sessions Wants to Revive." *Washington Post*, July 12, 2017. https://www.washingtonpost.com/news/wonk/wp/2017/07/12/a-brief-history-of-d-a-r-e-the-anti-drug-program-jeff-sessions-wants-to-revive/?utm_term=.1632ae0b2053.

Jonnes, Jill. *Hep-Cats, Narcs, and Pipe Dreams: A History of America's Romance with Illegal Drugs.* New York: Scribner's, 1996.

Katz, Josh. "Drug Deaths in America Are Rising Faster than Ever." *New York Times*, June 5, 2017. https://www.nytimes.com/interactive/2017/06/05/upshot/opioid-epidemic-drug-overdose-deaths-are-rising-faster-than-ever.html.

———. "The First Count of Fentanyl Deaths in 2016: Up 540% in Three Years." *New York Times,* September 2, 2017. https://www.nytimes.com/interactive/2017/09/02/upshot/fentanyl-drug-overdose-deaths.html.

Keller, Amy, RN, BSN. "How Much Does Heroin Cost?" DrugRehab.com, March 19, 2018. https://www.drugrehab.com/addiction/drugs/heroin/how-much-does-heroin-cost/#the-street-cost-of-heroin.

"Key Substance Use and Mental Health Indicators in the United States: Results from the 2016 National Survey on Drug Use and Health." Substance Abuse and Mental Health Services Administration, September 2017. https://www.samhsa.gov/data/sites/default/files/NSDUH-FFR1-2016/NSDUH-FFR1-2016.pdf.

Khatapoush, Shereen, and Denise Hallfors. "Sending the Wrong Message: Did Medical Marijuana Legalization in California Change Attitudes About and Use of Marijuana?" *Journal of Drug Issues*, Fall 2004.

Kovner, Guy. "Should Marijuana Be Legalized in California? A Look at Proposition 64." *Press Democrat* (Santa Rosa, CA), October 16, 2016. http://www.pressdemocrat.com/news/6179593-181/should-marijuana-be-legalized-in?sba=AAS.

Leduc, Diane, and James Lee. "Illegal Drugs and Drug Trafficking." Parliamentary Information and Research Services, 2003. http://www.parl.gc.ca/information/library/PRBpubs/bp435-e.htm.

Lopez, German. "How Fentanyl Became America's Leading Cause of Overdose Deaths." *Vox*, December 21, 2017. https://www.vox.com/science-and-health/2017/5/8/15454832/fentanyl-carfentanil-opioid-epidemic.

———. "Some Doctors Were Handing out Opioids like Candy. the Justice Department Just Shut Them Down." *Vox*, July 14, 2017. https://www.vox.com/policy-and-politics/2017/7/14/15968304/justice-department-opioid-epidemic.

———, ed. "The Spread of Marijuana Legalization, Explained." *Vox*, January 22, 2018. https://www.vox.com/cards/marijuana-legalization/where-is-marijuana-legal.

Luna, Erik. "Misguided Guidelines: A Critique of Federal Sentencing." *Policy Analysis,* November 1, 2002.

Mack, Alison, and Janet Joy. *Marijuana as Medicine? The Science Beyond the Controversy.* Washington, DC: National Academy Press, 2001.

Mai, Chris, and Ram Subramanian. "The Price of Prisons: Examining State Spending Trends, 2010–2015." Vera Institute of Justice,

May 2017. https://www.vera.org/publications/price-of-prisons-2015-state-spending-trends.

"Mandatory Minimum Penalties for Drug Offenses in the Federal Criminal Justice System." United States Sentencing Commission, October 2017. https://www.ussc.gov/sites/default/files/pdf/research-and-publications/research-publications/2017/20171025_Drug-Mand-Min.pdf.

"Mandatory Minimum Sentence Changes a Life." ABCNews. Accessed December 12, 2008. http://abcnews.go.com/Primetime/Story?id=356651&page=3.

"Mandatory Minimum Sentencing." Common Sense for Drug Policy. Accessed December 12, 2008. http://www.drugwarfacts.org/mandator.htm.

May, Channing. "Transnational Crime and the Developing World." Global Financial Integrity, March 2017. http://www.gfintegrity.org/wp-content/uploads/2017/03/Transnational_Crime-final.pdf.

McDonald, Bruce L. "*Board of Education v. Earls.*" Wiley Rein LLP, July 27, 2002. http://www.wileyrein.com/publication.cfm?publication_id=11590.

McGreal, Chris. "How Big Pharma's Money—and Its Politicians—Feed the US Opioid Crisis." *Guardian* (UK), October 19, 2017. https://www.theguardian.com/us-news/2017/oct/19/big-pharma-money-lobbying-us-opioid-crisis.

Mehta, Christine. "Why Drug Courts Are Not the Way Forward on America's Opioid Crisis." *Cornell Policy Review*, December 27,

2017. http://www.cornellpolicyreview.com/drug-courts-not-way-forward-americas-opioid-crisis.

"Methadone Maintenance Treatment," Drug Policy Alliance. Accessed December 12, 2008. http://www.lindesmith.org/library/research/methadone.cfm.

"Methadone Maintenance Treatment." *IDU HIV Prevention*, Centers for Disease Control and Prevention, February 2002. http://www.cdc.gov/IDU/facts/MethadoneFin.pdf.

"Mexico." US Department of State. Accessed March 28, 2018. https://paei.state.gov/j/inl/regions/westernhemisphere/219174.htm.

Miroff, Nick. "A Side Effect of Peace in Colombia? A Cocaine Boom in the U.S." *Washington Post*, May 8, 2017. https://www.washingtonpost.com/world/the_americas/a-side-effect-of-peace-in-colombia-a-cocaine-boom-in-the-us/2017/05/07/6fb5d468-294a-11e7-9081-f5405f56d3e4_story.html?utm_term=.51875b209149.

Mogensen, Jackie Flynn. "A Quick Guide to Legal Pot in California." *Mother Jones*, December 26, 2017. https://www.motherjones.com/politics/2017/12/a-quick-guide-to-legal-pot-in-california.

Moore, Solomon. "Trying to Break Cycle of Prison at Street Level." *New York Times,* November 23, 2007. https://www.nytimes.com/2007/11/23/us/23mapping.html.

"Morales' Controversial Coca Law Backed by Bolivian Court." *teleSUR*, November 11, 2017. https://www.telesurtv.net/english/

news/Morales-Controversial-Coca-Law-Backed-by-Bolivian-Court-20171111-0022.html.

Moskos, Peter. "Two Takes: Drugs Are Too Dangerous Not to Regulate; We Should Legalize Them." *US News and World Report*, August 7, 2008. https://www.usnews.com/opinion/articles/2008/07/25/two-takes-drugs-are-too-dangerous-not-to-regulate--we-should-legalize-them.

Murphy, Jenny, and Bryan Knowles. "Are Needle Exchange Programs a Good Idea?" SpeakOut.com. Accessed December 12, 2008. http://www.speakout.com/activism/issue_briefs/1352b-1.html.

Nadelmann, Ethan. "Drugs." *Foreign Policy*, September/October 2007.

"National Southwest Border Counternarcotics Strategy." Office of National Drug Control Policy, 2011. https://obamawhitehouse.archives.gov/sites/default/files/ondcp/policy-and-research/swb_counternarcotics_strategy11.pdf.

"Nation's Pediatricians Warn of Rising Risks to Youths from Loosening Marijuana Laws." American Academy of Pediatrics, February 27, 2017. https://www.aap.org/en-us/about-the-aap/aap-press-room/Pages/Nation%27s-Pediatricians-Warn-of-Rising-Risks-to-Youths-From-Loosening-Marijuana-Laws.aspx.

"Needle Exchange Facts." AIDS Action Policy Facts, June 2001. http://www.aidsaction.org/legislation/pdf/Policy_Facts-Needle_Exchange2.pdf.

"Needle Match." *Economist*, August 9, 2008. https://www.economist.com/node/11885792.

*New Jersey v. T.L.O.* 469 US 32 (1985).

"New York." Families Against Mandatory Minimums, 2016–2017. http://famm.org/states-map/new-york.

"91 Percent of Americans Support Criminal Justice Reform, ACLU Polling Finds." American Civil Liberties Union, November 16, 2017. https://www.aclu.org/news/91-percent-americans-support-criminal-justice-reform-aclu-polling-finds.

"Not Winning the War on Drugs." *New York Times*, July 2, 2008. https://www.nytimes.com/2008/07/02/opinion/02wed1.html.

O'Neill, Debra L., James M. Topolski, and W. Dean Klinkenberg. "Needle Exchange Programs: A Review of the Issues." Missouri Department of Health and Senior Services Office of Minority Health, September 27, 2004. http://mimh200.mimh.edu/mimhweb/pie/reports/Needle%20Exchange.pdf.

"Opioid Treatment Program Directory." Substance Abuse and Mental Health Services Administration. Accessed March 31, 2018. https://dpt2.samhsa.gov/treatment/directory.aspx.

Pelissier, Bernadette, Susan Wallace, Joyce Ann O'Neill, et al. "Prison Drug Program Outcomes." Federal Bureau of Prisons, 2001.

Peters, Jeremy W. "Albany Takes Step to Repeal Rockefeller Drug Laws." *New York Times,* March 4, 2009. https://www.nytimes.com/2009/03/05/nyregion/05rockefeller.html

"Pharmacy Owners Convicted of Illegally Selling 10 Million Hydrocodone Pills over the Internet," Drug Enforcement Administration, US Department of Justice, August 1, 2008. http://www.usdoj.gov/dea/pubs/states/newsrel/2008wdo080108.html.

Phippen, J. Weston. "Who Will Control Colombia's Cocaine Without FARC?" *Atlantic*, July 1, 2016. https://www.theatlantic.com/news/archive/2016/07/farc-cocaine-colombia/489551.

"Presidential Report." Office of National Drug Control Policy, 2002.

Public Safety Performance Project. "Voters Want Big Changes in Federal Sentencing, Prison System." Pew Charitable Trusts, February 12, 2016. http://www.pewtrusts.org/en/research-and-analysis/analysis/2016/02/12/voters-want-changes-in-federal-sentencing-prison-system.

"Quick Facts: Drug Trafficking Offenses." United States Sentencing Commission, 2016. https://www.ussc.gov/sites/default/files/pdf/research-and-publications/quick-facts/Quick_Facts_Drug_Trafficking_2016.pdf.

"Recidivism." Office of Justice Programs, National Institute of Justice, June 17, 2014. https://www.nij.gov/topics/corrections/recidivism/Pages/welcome.aspx.

"Recidivism Among Federal Drug Trafficking Offenders." United States Sentencing Commission, February 21, 2017. https://www.ussc.gov/research/research-reports/recidivism-among-federal-drug-trafficking-offenders.

Reitox National Focal Point. "Report to the EMCDDA: The Netherlands Drug Situation 2006." European Monitoring Centre for Drugs and Drug Addiction, October 2006.

"Results from the 2006 National Survey on Drug Use and Health: National Findings." Department of Health and Human Services, Substance Abuse and Mental Health Services Administration, Office of Applied Studies, September 2007. http://www.oas.samhsa.gov/nsduh/2k6nsduh/2k6Results.cfm.

Robinson, Melia, Jeremy Burke, and Skye Gould. "This Map Shows Every State That Has Legalized Marijuana." *Business Insider*, January 23, 2018. http://www.businessinsider.com/legal-marijuana-states-2018-1.

Rothwell, Jonathan. "How the War on Drugs Damages Black Social Mobility." Brookings, September 30, 2014. https://www.brookings.edu/blog/social-mobility-memos/2014/09/30/how-the-war-on-drugs-damages-black-social-mobility.

Rowe, Thomas. *Federal Narcotics Laws and the War on Drugs*. New York: Haworth Press, 2006.

"Safety for Use: Cannabis as a Gateway Drug." 2002 Petition to Reschedule Cannabis, DrugScience.org, 2002. http//www.drugscience.org/sfu/sfu_gateway.html.

Saunders, Nicole. "We Help Mothers Fighting Addiction Claim Their Voice." *Essence*, March 2005.

Scarborough, Rowan. "Heroin Traffic Finances bin Laden," *Washington Times*, December 6, 2004. http://www.house.gov/list/hearing/il10_kirk/afghanistandec6.html.

Schmidt, Kent J. "*United States v. Booker*: A Critical Change to the Federal Sentencing Guidelines." Dorsey and Whitney LLP, February 16, 2005. http://www.dorsey.com/Resources/Detail.aspx?pub=291.

Sebelius, Kathleen, Tommy G. Thompson, and Alan Weil. "Opioid Crisis: Five Ways to Tackle the US Drug Epidemic." BBC, August 6, 2017. http://www.bbc.com/news/world-us-canada-40479686.

Sher, George. "On the Decriminalization of Drugs." *Criminal Justice Ethics,* Winter/Spring 2003.

Shifter, Michael. "Latin America's Drug Problem." *Current History,* February 2007. http://www.currenthistory.com/Article.php?ID=453.

Siemaszko, Corky, "Sessions to End Legal Marijuana Policy from Obama Era." NBC News, January 4, 2018. https://www.nbcnews.com/storyline/legal-pot/sessions-end-obama-era-policy-legalized-marijuana-n834591.

"Snapshot: A Summary of CBP Facts and Figures." US Customs and Border Protection, March 2018. https://www.cbp.

gov/sites/default/files/assets/documents/2018-Mar/cbp-snapshot-20180320.pdf.

Solomon, Danyelle, and Connor Maxwell. "Substance Use Disorder Is a Public Health Issue, Not a Criminal Justice Issue." Center for American Progress, June 12, 2017. https://www.americanprogress.org/issues/race/news/2017/06/12/433998/substance-use-disorder-public-health-issue-not-criminal-justice-issue.

"State-By-State Medical Marijuana Laws." Marijuana Policy Project, 2008.

Steele, R. "The Cocaine Scene." *Newsweek*, May 30, 1977.

Steiner Broekhuysen, Erin. "Methadone." Office of National Drug Control Policy, Drug Policy Information Clearinghouse, April 2000. http://www.whitehousedrugpolicy.gov/publications/factsht/methadone/index/htm.

"Sterile Syringe Exchange Programs." Henry J. Kaiser Family Foundation, 2017. https://www.kff.org/hivaids/state-indicator/syringe-exchange-programs/?currentTimeframe=0&sortModel=%7B%22colId%22:%22Location%22,%22sort%22:%22asc%22%7D.

"Study: Mandatory Minimum Drug Sentences Don't Work." CNN Interactive, May 12, 1997. http://www.cnn.com/US/9705/12/mandatory.sentencing.

"Substance Abuse Treatment." Federal Bureau of Prisons. Accessed March 28, 2018. https://www.bop.gov/inmates/custody_and_care/substance_abuse_treatment.jsp.

"Substance Abuse Treatment." State of Delaware Department of Correction, December 27, 2006. http://www.doc.delaware.gov/Programs/treatmentprograms.shtml.

"Switzerland's Liberal Drug Policy Seems to Work, Study Says." *Medical Lexicon International,* June 2, 2006. http://www.medicalnewstoday.com/articles/44417.php.

"Syringe-Exchange Programs Effective in Reducing the Spread of AIDS." University of California Newsroom, July 26, 2001. http://www.universityofcalifornia.edu/news/article/3451.

"Syringe Services Programs." Centers for Disease Control and Prevention, February 27, 2018. https://www.cdc.gov/hiv/risk/ssps.html.

Tegel, Simeon. "Bolivia Ended Its Drug War by Kicking out the Dea and Legalizing Coca." *Vice News*, September 21, 2016. https://news.vice.com/article/bolivia-ended-its-drug-war-by-kicking-out-the-dea-and-legalizing-coca.

"Treatment Courts in the U.S.: Cutting Crime, Saving Money." National Association of Drug Court Professionals. Accessed March 28, 2018. http://www.nadcp.org/wp-content/uploads/2018/03/US-Drug-Court-Fact-Sheet.pdf.

"Understanding the Epidemic: Drug Overdose Deaths in the United States Continue to Increase in 2016." Centers for Disease

Control and Prevention, August 30, 2017. https://www.cdc.gov/drugoverdose/epidemic/index.html.

*United States v. Sokolow,* 490 US 1 (1989).

US Immigration and Customs Enforcement. "United States, Canada Announce Results of Operation Frozen Timber." *ICE* 3, no. 4 (2007). http://www.ice.gov/pi/news/insideice/articles/insideice_060725_web1.htm.

*Vernonia School District v. Wayne Acton,* 515 US 646 (1995).

Volknow, Nora D., M.D. "Measuring the Effectiveness of Drug Addiction Treatment." Testimony before the House Committee on Government Reform Subcommittee on Criminal Justice, Drug Policy, and Human Resources, March 30, 2004.

Wagner, Peter, and Wendy Sawyer. "Mass Incarceration: The Whole Pie 2018." Prison Policy Initiative, March 14, 2018. https://www.prisonpolicy.org/reports/pie2018.html.

Whiting, Penny F., Robert F. Wolff, Sohan Deshpande, et al. "Cannabinoids for Medical Use: A Systematic Review and Meta-analysis." *Journal of the American Medical Association* 313, No. 24 (June 23/30, 2015): 2456–2473. https://jamanetwork.com/journals/jama/fullarticle/2338251.

Zagaris, Bruce, and Scott Ehlers. "Drug Trafficking and Money Laundering." *Foreign Policy in Focus*, May 2001. http://www.fipif.org/fpiftxt/1416.

# Index

Page numbers in **boldface** are illustrations

addiction, 6–7, 14, 16, 20, 22–24, 32–34, 42, 44–45, 69, 74–75, 89–90, 93–95, 97–98, 101
Afghanistan, 15, 46, 50, 58–59, 62
AIDS, 23, 80, 90–91
al-Qaeda, 58–59
American Academy of Pediatrics (AAP), 79–80
American Medical Association, 28, 38, 80–81
Anslinger, Harry, 36–38, 40
Anti-Drug Abuse Act of 1986, 15, 19

Beats, 38–40
benzodiazepines, 8
Bolivia, 50–51, 56, 60–61
border smuggling, 10, 13, 15–16, 29, 54–55, 63
Bureau of Narcotics, 14, 36, 40–41

cannabis, 29, 79–80, 84
cartel, 45–46, 50, 56, 84

Coast Guard, **52**, 53–54
coca, 15, 32, 45, **46**, 51, 56–58, 60–**61**, 61, 84
cocaine, 8–9, 14–16, 20, 28, 31–34, 36, 43–46, 48, 50–51, **52**, 53–58, 60, 66, 68–69, 72, 80, 86, 100, 111, 115
coextensive, 107
Colombia, 15, 45–46, **46**, 50–51, 56–58
Controlled Dangerous Substances Act, 9, 43
counseling, **21**, 22, 93–95, 100–101
crack cocaine, 15, 48–50, **49**, 68–72, 111
crop eradication, 15, 51, 56–59, 62, 84

decriminalization, 14, 26, 78–80, 87, 92
defendant, 23, 47–48, 66–68, 72, 105
detoxification (detox), 101
disparities, 67, 69
drug court, 23, 72–75

Drug Enforcement
   Administration (DEA), 10,
   13, 54, 82–83, 111
drug-testing policies, 107,
   109–110

epidemic, 5–7, 10–11, 20,
   48–49, 68–70, 74

fentanyl, 10–11
Fourth Amendment rights, 25,
   **102**, 104, 107, 109–111,
   113–114

gateway drug, 8, 28, 80

harm-reduction programs, 18,
   21–22, 26, 75, 78, 90–91,
   93
Harrison Narcotics Act, 14,
   33–34
health effects, 45, 79, 83, 86,
   90
hepsters, 38–40
herbicide, 56–57, 62
heroin, 5–6, 8–11, 14–16, 22,
   28, 33–34, 36, 38, 40,
   42–44, 46–47, 50–51,
   54–57, 59, 66, 68, 75, 80,
   84, 86, 90, 93–95, 97, 115

HIV, 26, 90–93
hydrocodone, 23, 62

illicit, 8, 13, 16, 19, 23, 28, 31,
   63, 68–69, 78, 83–84,
   86–87, 110, 114–115
Immigration and Customs
   Enforcement (ICE), 54
incarceration, 26, 65, 69, 72, 89
intravenous, 90–91, 93

laudanum, 32
legalization, 8, 10, 14, 16–17,
   **18**, 26–29, 60, **76**, 78–80,
   83–87, 114
LSD, 9, 41–43, 68
lucrative, 59

mandatory minimums, 19,
   47–48, 66–68, 70–72
marijuana, 8–10, **9**, 14, 16–17,
   20, 26, 28–29, 38–39, 41,
   43–45, 47–48, 54–56, 68,
   78–84, **81**, 87, 99, 104,
   106, 114
McKesson Corporation, 7
medical use, 8–9, 28, 43,
   79–83, **81**, 87
methadone, 18, 22, 66, 68, 75,
   **92**, 93–96

methamphetamine, 8, 16, 54, 56, 74, 86
misconception, 95
misdemeanor, 68
money laundering, 62–63
morphine, 9, 14, 31–35, 37, 43, 93
muckrakers, 33

narcotic, 14, 31, 33–34, 36–37, 40–41, 50, 54, 57, 59–60, 101
National Association of Drug Court Professionals, 23, 74
National Institute on Drug Abuse, 21, 95, 97–98
needle-exchange programs, 18, 23, **26–27**, **88**, 90–93
Nixon, President Richard, 9, 14–15, 43–44

Office of National Drug Control Policy (ONDCP), 48, 50, 54–55
opioid, 5–8, 10–11, 15–16, 23–24, 26, 66, 75, 94
opium, 14–15, 32, 34, 36–37, 43, 46, 58–59, 62, 84, 94
overdose, 6–7, 10–11, 16, 26, 42, 45, 115
OxyContin, 62

parole, 68
patent medicine, **30**, 32–33
pharmaceutical companies, 6–7, 10, 24, 35
prescription drugs, 6–8, 10–11, 23–24, 26, 33, 62
prison sentence, 9–10, 15, 19, 43, 47, 65–66, 68, 70–74
Prohibition, 34–35, **35**, 37–38, 77, 85
Pure Food and Drug Act, 33

reasonable suspicion, 25, 105–106, 110–111, 113
recidivism, 20–21, 65, 74
recreational use, 8, 14, 16, 28, 79
rehabilitation, 17–18, 22–23, 67
Revolutionary Armed Forces of Colombia (FARC), 57, **58**
right to privacy, 103, 106–107, 109–110

scourge, 5
sentencing guidelines, 10, 47, 65–68, 71
speakeasy, 34–35, 38
stimulant, 40, 56

Taliban, 58–59

trafficking, 8, 13, 14–16, 18, 21, 40, 44–51, 54–55, 57, 59, 61–63, 65, 78, 83, 111, 113
treatment programs, 17–18, 21–23, **21**, 70, 73, 89, 93, **96**, 97, 100

US Customs and Border Protection, **9**, 15–16, 54–55
US Department of Health and Human Services, 6, 91
US Department of Justice, 24, 71

War on Drugs, 9, 14–15, 17–18, 25, 27, 29, 44, 47–48, 50–51, 53, 59–60, 68–69, 77–78, 83, 103, 110, 114
warrant, 25, 104–106, 110–111, 114
withdrawal, 6, 33, 44, 94–95

# About the Authors

**Richard Worth** is the author of more than sixty books, including biographies and books on history, politics, social issues, and current events. He has also written *Legal Gambling: Winner or Loser?* for Cavendish Square.

**Erin L. McCoy** is a literature, language, and cultural studies educator and an award-winning photojournalist and poet. She holds a master of arts degree in Hispanic studies and a master of fine arts degree in poetry from the University of Washington. She has edited nearly twenty nonfiction books for young adults, including *The Mexican-American War and The Israel-Palestine Border Conflict* from the Redrawing the Map series with Cavendish Square Publishing. She is from Louisville, Kentucky.